I ASK MY STUDENTS
"WHAT IS A PERFORMANCE?"

ARNOLD: "It's when you play onstage."
JASON: "It's going in front of people and doing what you do."
JENNIFER: "It's entertaining people by showing them your talent."

Those are good answers, but they all indicate that a performer is doing something "to" an audience. I don't view it quite that way.

Rather, I think of a performance as a conversation between you and an audience. A conversation based on listening, with the knowledge that the best conversations are the results of *taking in,* as opposed to putting out.

A performance is a conversation that begins when you go onstage, take in all that's happening around you, get a sense of where you are and how you feel, and then react to that reality.

Since it is a conversation, there will probably be a response to what you do—although there are no guarantees, as you'll see. If the audience likes what you've done, do it again. If they don't, do something else. Of course, sometimes it's impossible to tell if they like it. Heck, sometimes the audience can't tell.

Don't worry about this confusion. This book is about having belief in yourself and developing confidence in your value as a person, learning to be free of fear and open in front of all those people.

STAGE
Performance

LIVINGSTON TAYLOR

POCKET BOOKS
New York   London   Toronto   Sydney   Singapore

An *Original* Publication of POCKET BOOKS

 POCKET BOOKS, a division of Simon & Schuster Inc.
1230 Avenue of the Americas, New York, NY 10020

ISBN: 0-671-03971-7

First Pocket Books trade paperback printing March 2000

10 9 8 7 6 5 4 3 2 1

POCKET and colophon are registered trademarks of Simon & Schuster Inc.

Book design by Laura Lindgren and Celia Fuller

Cover design by Anna DeRoos
Front cover photo by Chuck Pefley

Printed in the U. S. A.

*To my wife, Maggie, whose beauty makes me look good,
and whose intelligence makes me seem bright*

CONTENTS

All Things in Good Time 41

Reality 57

Great Expectations 69

Radio and TV and the Magic of "B S P" 83

ACKNOWLEDGMENTS

This book is dedicated to Charles Koppelman, whose love of the great song and affection for me kept me afloat through my grim late twenties and early thirties.

To Don Law, whose unshakeable moral compass and sense of fairness have allowed him to sail successfully in some very rough show business seas, for giving me a first-hand view of what happens on a storm-tossed deck.

To Donna Roll, a teacher whose technical knowledge of voice is coupled with a complete understanding of the underlying heart and soul that drive the need to sing.

To Rob Rose, the unofficial mayor of the Berklee College of Music, who brought me into the classroom because he believed I might have something to teach.

And to Shelly Schultz, the quintessential agent who softened the harsh lessons of show biz with a secret stash of love and compassion.

With special thanks to Parker Bartlett, who started the process of editing this book, and to Nancy Fitzpatrick whose good humor, patience, and uncanny ability to decipher my handwriting have made this project not just possible, but one of my more pleasant experiences.

To John Boylan, passionate student, patient teacher, and proofreader extraordinaire. To Dan Strone, who led me to Jane Cavolina, whose advocacy and tenacity found this book a home.

STAGE
Performance

INTRODUCTION

I'm the curious type. Born that way. Why is water wet? What keeps a plane in the air? Why does glass shatter? Why is stone so hard? Why does gold shine and iron rust? I've spent countless gentle hours thinking about gravity and how it might be controlled. And I'm at my best when I'm straining to observe it all—squishy earthworms, gray-green moss, lightbulbs, bacteria, doorknobs, paramecium, firebrick, mushrooms, faded wood, indelible ink, bamboo. Born a camera, photographing my instant of consciousness. That curiosity brings us to this book.

I teach a performance class at the Berklee College of Music in Boston, a school that's been in existence for fifty years and is well known as the foremost jazz and contemporary music school in the country.

I love being around my students at Berklee. Twentysomething is a great age—just aware enough to have the entire mountain range in view, and energetic and naive enough to believe it can, in fact, be crossed.

Let me introduce you to the thirteen students who represent this semester's class. They are Jason, Kathy, Boris, Arnold, Charlotte, Laura, Dustin, Krystal, Jennifer, Lee, Trevor, Tim, and Phil. Although all the students are real, they never actually existed in one class at one time. They are a composite of the six hundred or so students I have taught.

As the semester progresses, you'll get to know them in more detail. For now, understand that they represent the most diverse assemblage I could imagine in one place at one time. They arrive at Berklee from all over the world, from all economic and educational backgrounds, with one thing in common: a consuming desire to have their musical and philosophical ideas heard and recognized. They've been told by everyone who loves them that there are easier paths to walk. Some eventually will have to take the easier path, but right now they need to explore the limit of what is possible, and I am extremely excited to help them try.

I call my assemblage of students a class, although that's not quite accurate. It's more of a laboratory where, for two hours for two sections each Tuesday, we experiment and explore what it means to present yourself and your vision to other people.

This book exists because so much information flies around the class that it's impossible to take it all in at once. I wanted my students to have something to refer back to long after the semester was over and as their careers evolved. I also wanted others intent on developing confidence to have a place to turn, to hear the ramblings of a veteran of the performance wars.

The random nature of my Stage Performance class (not to mention my life) convinced me that the only way to organize this book was to tape a semester of lectures and class performances, and use the tapes as a reminder of what happened on any given day. Although there is a vague course outline, I'm content to let each class (like my shows) follow its own course, and I encourage/demand active student participation. Also, rather than force this book into some rigid framework, the chapters spring from the snapshot of the moment. Although reading the book front to back is fine, feel free to let it fall open where it may and dig in.

LIVINGSTON TAYLOR

WHAT IS A
PERFORMANCE?

I was sixteen years old and in genuine trouble. The chaos of my brain was crashing into the demands of ordered, functional society, and the situation was causing enormous pain. I was at war with school, a battle that had begun years earlier when I was forced to repeat third grade. As a result, my study habits were nonexistent, my grades were terrible, and I wound up in an alternative high school west of Boston where the doors were locked and the students had no keys.

Music has always been a large part of my existence. Early on, I found sanity in the discipline of rhythm and the order of chords and melody. Singing is actually organized shouting, and the organized shouting of song and lyrics wicked away much local pain.

I recall, as though it were yesterday, the instant I realized music was going to be my way out. It was a clear, cold early March day, and I was in transit. My status in the "school" had risen to the point where I was free to move between buildings unescorted. En route, I took a moment to look up into a painfully blue sky. The clarity of the day drifted into my thoughts.

Whenever I've gotten in trouble, I've been able to float above myself and rationally peer over the horizon into the future. On that clear March day, as I looked down at my situation from that lofty position, I realized academia wasn't an option. And, at 130 pounds soaking wet, with occasional asthma, physical labor seemed a stretch. Yup, no doubt about it. Music was going to be my way out. It was, I believed, the only way out.

So I went back to my dorm room, picked up my guitar, and went to work.

More than four thousand performances over more than thirty years, a dozen CDs, hundreds of songs, acting jobs, TV hosting, commercial singing and writing, and just about every other experience in show business have given me a few thoughts on what's happening out there.

I ask my students, "What is a performance?"

ARNOLD: "It's when you play onstage."
JASON: "It's going in front of people and doing what you do."
JENNIFER: "It's entertaining people by showing them your talent."

Those are good answers, but they all indicate that a performer is doing something "to" an audience. I don't view it quite that way.

Rather, I think of a performance as a conversation between you and an audience. A conversation based on listening, with the knowledge that the best conversations are the result of *taking in*, as opposed to putting out.

A performance is a conversation that begins when you go onstage, take in all that's happening around you, get a sense of where you are and how you feel, and then react to that reality.

Since it is a conversation, there will probably be a response to what you do—although there are no guarantees, as you'll see. If the audience likes what you've done, do it again. If they don't, do something else. Of course, sometimes it's impossible to tell if they like it. Heck, sometimes the audience can't tell.

Don't worry about this confusion. This book is about having belief in yourself and developing confidence in your value as a person, learning to be free of fear and open in front of all those people.

Now, listen. What do you hear?

STUDENTS: "Traffic."
"A bass from another classroom."
"Ventilation."
"Voices in the hall."

All of the external noises are as much a part of a performance as anything else. They are always present in varying degrees. Listen to the noise that already exists and think of how you can adjust your own noise so that it fits in with the environment.

To acclimate yourself to the externals, take some time onstage before you begin a performance—again, taking in before you put out. In other words, notice and pay attention to everything that's happening around you. First, be patient. Don't let nervousness jump-start your performance and force you to begin before you're ready. Breathe in. Breathe out. Wait. Watch your audience. Listen to them. Be still. Patience and stillness are very inviting rooms.

I love silence. I'm a connoisseur of silence. And the most important thing about silence is not that the audience can hear you, but that *you can hear them.*

Sometimes their communication is quite clear. "Yo, bucko! You stink! Get off the stage!" But usually they communicate displeasure with more subtlety. However they do it, they send continual signals, and if you're lucky, there will be enough silence around to hear what they're saying.

Also, remember the acronym K.I.S.S. (Keep It Simple, Students.) I always play simply enough so that I have plenty of room to respond to the unexpected outside stimulus: people entering the hall; a spilled drink; a siren in the street.

Room to react tells an audience that you're in the moment. I always watch my audience, and when the lights are in my eyes, I listen to them. To the rustle of corduroy. The creak of a chair. The cough of boredom. All are part of the conversation of performance. I speak fluent "audience-ese." When it is really quiet in an auditorium, I can whisper onstage and be heard by the people in the top balcony as though I were next to them.

My job onstage is to look and to listen, to identify problems, and, whenever possible, to solve them. Sometimes I'm the right guy in the wrong place and nothing I do works. For that particular audience, I will be terrible. It happens.

When I'm onstage my top priority is not technique, style, or passion. My top priority is to perform with total awareness. I'm watching and listening all the time because I need information from my audience. How are they doing? Are they okay?

If you're an amazing singer, songwriter, or instrumentalist, you may not have to worry as much about your audience. Your talent may shine so brightly it will more than compensate for any lack of audience attention. But you need to ask yourself, "How good am I? Am I good enough in one area to ignore weaknesses in other areas?" I don't know about you, but I'm not good enough to be commercially successful firing on seven cylinders. I need all eight.

There are performers out there who take beautiful care of their audiences. A short time ago, I attended Jimmy Buffett's concert at the Great Woods Center in Mansfield, Massachusetts. Jimmy had sold out all four nights at Great Woods, with twenty thousand people in the venue each night—a total of eighty thousand people, at an average of $30 per ticket. That's right, $2.4 million gross in ticket sales. Wow!

Now is Jimmy Buffett great-looking? Is he a great singer? He's only had modest Top Ten radio airplay ("Come Monday" and "Margaritaville"). So what explains his success? I'll tell you what I think. I think he's having that conversation with his audience—all the time. A give-and-take. Action and reaction.

I was there on the third of the four nights, and at one point during the show, Jimmy looked out at the crowd and said, "Last night, I thought we had gotten just about as crazy as we could get. But, darn, you people are about to prove me wrong!" The crowd went wild. They went wild because Jimmy made them feel important. He made them believe that they had a direct influence on the course of the show; that their enthusiasm, under his watchful eye, would be of great value in the show's success. Whenever he performs, Jimmy keeps a watch on his audience. He smiles at them and is genuinely concerned that they enjoy themselves.

When he walks onstage he surveys the crowd and then welcomes them. "Good evening, everybody." He speaks slowly. (The larger the crowd, the slower you talk.) "It is so great to be...back...at Great Woods." Here, there's a slight pause, at which point Jimmy breathes in and says, "In . . ." Now the audience is totally on edge. Does Buffett know where he is? Of course he does, but he's not quick to relieve the tension. Finally, he blurts out ". . . Mansfield, Massachusetts."

There is relieved, ecstatic pandemonium. Why? It's simple. Because Jimmy could accurately identify his exact location, as opposed to a vague "the Boston area" or "New England." This told the audience that he was completely aware of his exact location and it allowed them to abandon their reality and enter his. Because he was able to prove that he knew exactly where he was, it seemed reasonable to let him captain the ship.

As a performer it's easy to believe that you are the reason why people are enjoying themselves. After all, each of us is pretty important to ourselves. As individual performers, Livingston Taylor, Jimmy Buffett, Sarah McLachlan, et al, are actually minor catalysts around which an audience builds an experience. What happens is that people will see that Livingston Taylor (or Jimmy Buffett or whoever) is playing at a local club on Friday night. Carol and Sam will get together with Jack and Betty, get in their car, have dinner, and go to the show. Although the performance was the catalyst for getting together, our part in their evening was certainly less important than their time together as friends. On their way home, they'll discuss the performance, whether it was good or bad, better or worse than a previous time. Maybe my voice was a little scratchy. Maybe I was a bit tired in the beginning. As I said, we're a major part of our own lives, but a remarkably minor part of the audience's.

Please remember: Your audience means a lot more to you than you mean to them.

N-E-R-V-O-U-S-N-E-S-S

This "sense of our own importance" brings up another issue—nervousness. I ask my students if any of them get nervous before they perform. Every hand rises except John's. He explains he's too nervous to raise his hand.

What does it feel like to be nervous?

KATHY: "Short of breath. Stomachache. Have to go to the bathroom. Knees shake. Palms are sweaty. And I've forgotten what I'm supposed to do."

Who are you thinking about when you're nervous? Your audience, the people you're working for? I think not. When you're badly nervous, you're only thinking about *yourself*, and the discomfort you're in. This is the problem with nervousness. You should be paying close attention to your audience. You should be having "the conversation" but you can't. Your fear forces total self-centeredness.

You get nervous because you're afraid and worried you'll make a fool of yourself, that something unexpected will surface and put you in a situation where you'll be out of control.

Let's look at this a bit. What's the worst that can happen onstage?

JENNIFER: "You can be really bad. Terrible."
ARNOLD: "Completely forget your part."
TREVOR: "Have your fly down."

Sometimes the worst does happen, and in spite of your best efforts and wishes, you wind up being *absolutely awful*.

I want you to know I've been *absolutely awful* many times. I've played on a stage where the entire audience "booed" me at the top of their lungs, sometimes simply because I was, once again, the right guy in the wrong place.

How does it feel to be absolutely awful? Let's qualify it. What's the common phrase that people use to describe being terrible onstage?

PHIL: "I died."

In spite of how it feels, has anyone actually died from being terrible onstage? Of course not. So let's figure out how bad it really is so we know what we're actually going to face. Have you ever stubbed your toe? Hard? Stupefying pain for a couple of minutes. Have you ever broken a bone? Yes? It hurt and inconvenienced you for weeks or months.

Well, I've stubbed my toe hard plenty of times and I've broken both arms and a leg (the result of a raucous childhood). Being awful onstage is worse than stubbing your toe really hard but not as bad as breaking a bone. It hurts, but you get over it, and the damage isn't likely to be permanent.

Being fearful of being "absolutely awful" is detrimental to your performance, but how do you get out of it? First, you've got to see your audience—with every sense available to you. At the risk of bruising your ego, they don't care how you feel about yourself. They have given you their time and money and they expect you to pay attention to them. They don't want you to be self-absorbed; they want you to concentrate on them. Now these are probably decent people who will be sympathetic and supportive if they see that you are in distress. But what they want is to have a good time. To suspend their reality and enter yours. To laugh, to cry, to be part of the reality that you, as an entertainer, are creating.

They want attention, and they want to feel that their presence is special to you, that it makes a difference in the course of events that make up your show. They want to believe you are glad to be with them.

If you're focused on yourself and caught up in nervousness, you're taking attention away from your audience—the attention they want and deserve, the same attention that is returned to you in the form of their participation in your performance. Their attention is a gift. Don't throw it away. Even if you think you don't deserve it, receive that gift graciously. "Thank you for your energy. Your presence is a beautiful compliment."

Now let's talk about another essential ingredient in your career. I ask the class who would like to be a professional musician, singer, actor?

All hands rise.

What comes to mind when you hear the word *professional*?

BORIS: "It's what somebody does for a living."

"Professional—for a living." This phrase indicates that someone is getting paid, that they are making M-O-N-E-Y. If your music isn't making money, it will become your hobby. If your art can support you, you'll be able to spend most of your time doing what you love—making music, creating your art.

Before we go further, let's define what money really is: Money is a mutually agreed upon item of value that makes life convenient. It is not bad or evil. It is simply *value given for value received*. Payment for performance. It's possible to do a show where all ten members of the audience are so pleased that they invite you to their houses for breakfast the next morning. The problem is, you have ten offers and you can only eat one breakfast. What's the solution? Eat one breakfast and let the other nine people give you three dollars each so you can eat on subsequent mornings.

One of my students asks, "Livingston, what are the chances that I can make a living making music?" If your needs are simple, your chances are good. If you're looking for externals to fix a broken inside, there will never be enough.

In the performing arts, where does the money come from? What is its ultimate source?

LEE: "Record companies."
TIM: "Club owners and promoters."

Nice answers, but they're not quite accurate.

You'll find great fantasies at work when you think of how you'll get successful: "If I could just get a big manager to hear my music." "If I could just get a record company to sign me." Have you had similar fantasies about your life? Sure. You have them all the time. I certainly do. "Darn. If I could just get discovered, I'd be home free. If I could just get that one big break." Have you tried that one on yourself? I have. The knight in shining armor to rescue you from yourself.

I want to give you the bad news right away. You're not going to be discovered. It has never happened in the past. It is not going to happen today. Nor will it happen in the future. No one is ever "discovered" and rocketed to fame. From a distance it may appear that way, but on close examination, you'll see that successful careers are actually a mix of perseverance, intelligence, and talent (okay, and a skosh of luck).

The source of all money in the music industry is *the audience*. It is made up of individuals who have decided that your art has value. The audience pays your salary. They are the foundation of your career. Record companies, managers, and agents, although important, do not generate income directly (at least not for long). The only enduring source of support for a career is an audience.

So now we get to the essence: *how to develop and care for an audience.*

Don't despair. You've already been given a huge break. As my friend Christine Lavin says, "A goober and a squiggly got together." They got together and created you. The chances of your being here right now were infinitesimally small, but it happened. You won the lottery. You were born. However, your career is not a lottery, or the product of random chance. What your career is—and what it will be—is the result of the cultivation, care, and feeding of the people who pay your salary: your audience. The good news is that you don't have to be discovered. Showing up each day, clear and observant, will be enough.

Your career is in your hands, and making it happen is a doable deed.

Do Something

One of the main things I want to emphasize is the idea of flexibility. Not waiting for things to line up properly but moving ahead with what you've got right now. I like controlled movement, even in the wrong direction. Parts that move don't rust and freeze.

There is no rule book for your career. It's going to be made up as you go along. So don't get lost in the fantasy of how your career should be. Have your heroes and your influences. These are wonderful beacons to follow when the road gets dark. But your career will not be Madonna's or John Coltrane's, or Phish's. Nor are their careers necessarily as wonderful as you may believe. Remember, you're seeing them through the distorted filters of the entertainment media (*Rolling Stone,* MTV, etc.). You're also going to hear a lot of rumor and supposition about how various people got where they are. Just don't expect to follow their path. Information drawn from mass media is notoriously incomplete. You don't really know about these artists' careers. You can and should admire and critique others, but your career, by its very nature, will be unique to you.

Let the Performance Begin

Since a good conversation often begins with an introduction, the first thing I have my students do is introduce themselves around the class with an appropriate exchange of names and a good strong handshake, all the while maintaining eye contact. After that, I have them step onto the stage at the front of the room and introduce themselves, one at a time.

STUDENT: "Hello, my name is Trevor Lancet."

(Trevor is a lanky twenty-year-old with long hair and tight pants. He is a guitar major with Bon Jovi–type rock and roll dreams. Unexpectedly alone without his guitar, he flushes with fear. His body tension reminds me of frozen cardboard.)

LIVINGSTON: "Where is Trevor looking right now?"
PHIL: "At you."
LIVINGSTON: "Why is he looking at me?"
PHIL: "Well, you're the teacher."

LIVINGSTON: "Yes, but I am also just another member of Trevor's audience, even though it probably is a good idea to shoot a glance my way. I am, after all, passing out grades at the end of the semester. But what about the rest of the crowd? He should be looking at them and trying to actually *see* them. Looking at the audience is the most basic way of telling them that you're paying attention to them."

As we continue the introductions, I ask the class to pay close attention to the person onstage. A performer sends out signals and messages. And the audience sends them messages and makes continual decisions about a performer. Literally volumes of nonverbal communication are going back and forth every instant: the tension of the arms, the tilt of the head, the depth of breath, closeness of the shave, cut of the clothes. These and thousands of other cues are instantly transferred to and absorbed by the audience.

Laura balks. "I don't judge people by first glance," she says.

I try to explain the difference between judging and responding. Let's walk down the street. Each person we see generates a response in us. The business person's clean-cut suit, the carefree flow of a student released from class, the oblivion of a chatty group of close friends, the alarm triggered by a street person passed out at an odd angle in a doorway. Judgments based on first impressions are not bad. It is responsible behavior. That said, we hopefully have the capacity for reassessment as more information about a person becomes available.

I'm amused by the arrogant reporter who demands to know why a voter did or did not support a politician. When forced to make a verbal response to nonverbal information, it's often painfully simplistic. "Uh, I don't like the way he cuts his hair"—prompting outcries of supposed voter ignorance. Nothing could be further from the truth. The spoken part of our reaction to other people is small indeed, and I believe that people are remarkably capable at collecting nonverbal information, and wise in their assessment of their fellow man.

I say to the class: In the delivery of nonverbal information to your audience, I want you to follow a predictable order.

1. Walk onstage.
2. Face the crowd.
3. Find a spot where you're comfortable.
4. Be still and see your audience.
5. Say your name. (This is the performance.)
6. Be still and look at the audience. Make sure they received what you gave out.
7. Bow slightly.
8. Accept applause, if appropriate.
9. Leave the stage.

I ask them: "When Trevor was in front of you, did you form opinions about him? Of course, you did. Every person we see conveys to us, in a split second, a dictionary's worth of information about themselves." That's not to say our opinions of people can't or won't change, it just recognizes that first impressions are inevitable.

In all the time that you're onstage during this fifteen-second introduction, saying your name is the only verbal component of the performance, and it takes up only a couple of seconds. In spite of the brevity of the "performance" (saying your name), you have imparted a huge quantity of information to your audience.

The introductions continue. "Hello, my name is Kathy Walls."

What did you learn from Kathy during that introduction?

Arnold, a good-humored Brooklyn, New York, native, zeroes in on her accent. "She's from the South." The class is much amused that with his own distinct accent, he should remark on hers.

Did any of you notice how Kathy walked onstage and kept moving? How she never stopped? Never took a moment to be still?

More than anything else, stillness is essential to establishing control. Stillness is the straight line, the horizon from which all the angles and curves of a performance flow. Stillness allows an audience to observe you and become familiar with your externals. Once comfortable with the outside, the chances of their accepting what's on the inside improve.

Being onstage is like playing a grown-up game of Simon Says. If you are tense, your audience will be tense. If you are still and at ease, your audience will be still and at ease.

The audience wants to enter your reality. If your reality is nervous and agitated, it will exhaust them. At some point they'll have to turn away to rest. As your panic level rises, it can be seen and read by your audience, who see rigid shoulders and arms, shallow breathing, wide eyes, a clenched jaw. All these things say you are ill at ease. Conversely, if your arms and shoulders are relaxed and your breathing smooth and steady, it will tell your audience that you are at ease.

Lee, a trumpet major from Taiwan, raises his hand with a most concerned look. "Please, Mr. Taylor, does this matter for me?"

I think, absolutely. The rules of engaging your audience

apply regardless of the instrument played. From operatic singing to the washboard, you must be still, look, and observe; take in, before putting out.

An important component of nervousness is expectation, that is, what might happen? Let's see how much trouble we can get into with expectations.

"Who has had the experience of rehearsing in their rooms, thinking that their music sounds pretty good, only to get onstage and have it completely fall apart?"

All hands rise.

It's amazing that the same piece of music can be so good in one place and so terrible in another. It's no wonder performers get nervous. They never know when they are going to be blindsided. Here's what happens. Performers in one environment develop a series of expectations about what will happen elsewhere. They carry those expectations onstage, and when a show doesn't go as expected, panic sets in and the house of cards (aka their fantasy of how things were supposed to go) crumbles.

Expectations and assumptions are like tree stumps in the dark. They are ready, willing, and able to help you stub your toes. It is terrible to panic onstage. You get offstage. You cry. Your friends (other than the ones who snuck out the back door) tell you that you weren't that bad. (That means you were pretty bad.) Then your mother tells you that you weren't that bad. Guess what? That means you were absolutely awful. Let's find a way to stay in ourselves and avoid panic.

It is tough to believe that you have the right to be onstage, that you have the right to be still and at ease until your surroundings are evaluated and you are ready to proceed. To believe you have this right doesn't come overnight. I've been at it for over thirty years and I still struggle with my right to be onstage. But I do work on it.

The moment you walk through the door of the place where you are going to perform, you send out signals about who you are and what you are about. You cannot turn yourself on and off. You are a continuum.

In the early part of my career I often struggled with my right to be onstage. It's surprising where the permission came from. It was in the fall of 1976, and my career had been in a downhill drift since the disappointing sales of my last Capricorn Records release, *Over the Rainbow*. With no record contract, and shrinking audiences, I was beginning to have serious doubts about whether I should remain an entertainer. The light at the end of the tunnel was faint indeed. Then one afternoon I got a phone call from a fellow named Ian Anderson. Ian is the head of a British group called Jethro Tull with whom I had toured extensively in the early 1970s. Ian asked me a favor. He was not feeling well and had two sold-out shows to do at Madison Square Garden in New York. He wanted to know if I would be the opening act for these two shows. I was complimented he had chosen to call me, but I told him I had reservations. It was my sense that his audience had become quite rabid over the years and that they would probably kill me if I were to attempt, as the opening act, to delay their reunion with their favorite band, Jethro Tull. However, remembering my financial situation, I asked Ian what he would be paying. The reply: $1,000 a night. With a stack of unpaid bills in clear sight, my mind changed easily. I'd be there that afternoon.

Showtime came and the Garden was packed. My name was announced, and as I stepped to center stage, alone with my guitar, I was greeted with a chorus of boooos so thick, low, and aggressive, I thought I'd drown. So there I was, a guy at the end of his career, being booed by sixteen thousand pimply-faced, chemically altered male adolescent slugs. In the midst of that din and self-doubt, a remarkable thing happened. As I played my first song, and accepted the reality of the audience's displeasure, a calm and a clarity came over me. I was onstage and I was ready to be there. I belonged there. That sixteen thousand people adamantly disagreed made no difference. It was their problem. I could see and hear their clear disappointment with my presence, and although it made me sad that they were saying no to what I had to offer, it did nothing to change the fact that I was where I belonged. It was they who were in the wrong place, not me.

It's taken a number of years of hindsight to be able to articulate what happened that night. At the time, my response was harsher. As the boos rose to a crescendo and the clarity came over me, I stopped playing, looked at the audience, and spoke clearly into the microphone. "Ian Anderson and Jethro Tull are here tonight. In about twenty minutes they're going to be out here and they're going to be *fantastic*." The crowd went wild. "But right now, I'm here, and if you don't like it, you can *get out*." Oh, boy, were they mad. Nonetheless, I finished my fifteen minutes.

When I got offstage, Ian Anderson came up to me and remarked that my show had been a pretty tough go. I agreed with his dry, English understatement. Knowing that we had one more night of this, and in an attempt to reassure me that the worst was over, Ian explained that the next night would be easier because the second night was the second show that had gone on sale. Certainly, the fans would be less rabid. You can predict what happened. The second night was, in fact, the *first* night to have gone on sale, and when I hit the stage, they were ready for me. The opening boo was a third again as loud as anything I had heard the night before, and this audience added a couple of twists. As I was playing my first song, a sparkle to the right caught my eye. It was an empty pint bottle of whiskey on its way to the stage. It smashed, and the glass drifted around my feet. Tull was so popular at the time that they had sold the seats behind the stage: 360 degrees of people committed to kicking a little folk heinie. A long-neck beer bottle floated through the spotlights, missed me by inches, and went into the audience out front. Simultaneously, a cherry bomb exploded in the deep left side of the hall.

Now I had a problem. My presence onstage was putting my audience at risk. In spite of my feelings about them (which were quite negative) they were, nonetheless, my audience; and as my audience, they were my responsibility. That my presence was putting them in danger was intolerable. I broke my rhythm, stilled my strings, looked out at them and announced that it was impossible to continue. After a curt bow I left the stage.

From that low point, my career fortunately ticked upward with a record contract with a major label and some good solid public acceptance of the music I was making. It's drifted up and down many times since Madison Square Garden but always with the sense that, for better or worse, I've earned my right to be onstage.

The students continue their performances—introducing themselves and dutifully following my prescribed order for being onstage. After the names, I have them follow the same routine by reciting the alphabet. After ten minutes or so of the alphabet performance, I explain that despite the sophomoric nature of the exercise, their reciting of the alphabet is, in fact, a real performance and that in spite of its simplicity, large quantities of nonverbal conversation are taking place between the performer and the audience.

Phil asks plaintively, "When are we going to get to play our music?"

I respond, "Not as soon as you want, but soon enough. Probably in a couple of weeks. But be patient. I want your performances to stand on a solid foundation, and it takes some time to understand what that foundation is all about, and to be comfortable with it. Your assignment for next week is to memorize one or two minutes' worth of prose or poetry and be ready to recite it."

Their sighs are "music to my ears." They tell me that, although skeptical, they are willing to listen to, and for the time being, follow my vision of performance.

CRAWL,
THEN WALK

Good morning, class. Once again, for me, what is a performance?

"It's a conversation between an audience and a performer."

And who pays a performer's salary?

"The audience."

And why does an audience give a performer money?

"Because they want to."

That's right. And, I don't mean money as in a guitar-shaped swimming pool. I mean money as *value given* for value received.

Have any of you seen any big shows recently?

"Tom Petty. Phish. U2. Steely Dan."

Ooh, Steely Dan at Harbor Lights? Were they good? Good sound and lights? I would guess they played all the hits. And how about the crowd? Sold-out? I bet.

Was Jeff Baxter there, playing guitar? If you're not sure, he probably wasn't. I know Jeff well. In the early 1980s he coproduced an album for me, and he likes to make his presence known. How many people at Harbor Lights? Ten thousand? All paying an average of $25 per ticket? What's the gross on that? Yeah, $250,000. Hello! That's a lot of money.

What can Steely Dan afford, if they're grossing $250,000 a night? Great travel and food; super sound and lights; roadies to set up and break down the stage; lighting and stage designers, limousines, and lots of rooms in good hotels. In short, they'll have plenty of money to finance a world-class tour.

Now, what can club owners or promoters expect to make from you guys? What are your names presently worth?

PHIL (shaking his head): "Not much."

Sadly, at this early point in your career, it's true. Because you have yet to develop an audience base, your names are worth little to a promoter. And because of what you can earn, which is almost nothing in comparison to acts such as Aerosmith, Dave Matthews, or Billy Joel, you have very little power to demand much from club owners or promoters. You need to expect and prepare for terrible sound systems, surly club staffs, crummy (sometimes nonexistent) lights, and generally indifferent treatment. Without an audience to finance you, your power base cannot help but be small. Don't fret. Rather than lamenting the situation, let's figure out how to work with what you've got, to make that audience grow.

The very fact that an artist is on MTV or Top Forty radio means they've developed a strong power base. That's good for them, but don't be confused. They are not you.

As I've said before, your career is unique to you. It doesn't matter how Elvis, Billy Joel, or U2 did it. Be influenced, emulate, and admire them, but don't compare yourself to them. Understand that their careers are not yours, and that trying to design your career after watching them or anyone you admire on MTV or in any other performance venue is like building a house after looking at a lightbulb.

The nature of the business dictates that your career gets made up as you go along. Flexibility and adaptability will be your keys to success. Pontificating on an unknown future is a monumental waste of time. It's much better to observe and react.

Your career is not what you "put out." It's not in fancy guitars, weird haircuts, or big breaks. It's not what goes out, but what you can take in. Your eyes, ears, sense of touch, taste, and smell all plug into your greatest career asset: *your brain.* This is where your career and success come from. Not from your heart, your soul, your makeup, or your instrument, but from your ability to process what's happening around you and to realistically assess where you are and what you have to work with. The ability to adjust will be a repeating theme throughout your career.

Making Do with What You've Got

In the late 1970s, I did a tour with Linda Ronstadt, a wonderful singer and a good friend. On this tour, she carried a B3 organ that she used on *one* love song. She was making enough money to go ahead and absorb a refrigerator-size piece of equipment for one song. Doodads are difficult and expensive to carry. They require the kind of time and attention that can distract you from your boss—your audience. You and I do not have those resources, but we do have brains, and we need to use them.

When I travel and do shows, I like to use what's around me. If you go camping, you can either bring fuel and a stove with you, or you can bring a pack of matches and when you get to your campsite, pick up sticks, strike a match, make a fire, and using what's already there, cook that hot dog.

Please remember: Stay lean and simple, and avoid gimmicks. Concentrate all your resources on building an audience base.

Who Are You?

When I play, the first thing I do is show up early and introduce myself to as many people as I can—sound people, waitstaff, janitors, bartenders, anyone remotely connected with the show. I tell them my name and explain that I'm the person scheduled to play that night.

Say your name, early and often. Names are important. If people don't know your name, how will they find you again, to buy your CD, come to a show, or tell their friends about you? *Never* assume that someone knows who you are. You will embarrass them and eventually yourself.

In the early 1970s I did a few shows with the rock group Emerson Lake & Palmer. At the sound check before our first show there was a person playing piano. Was it Keith Emerson? Or just a roadie? I didn't know, and he didn't introduce himself. I felt awkward and worried. In my unsettled condition, I made a promise to myself. I would never assume that somebody would know who I am. I always introduce myself.

There is a TV newswoman in Boston named Liz Walker. Although we've known each other for many years, our paths cross infrequently. Each time I see her I reintroduce myself, and she always exclaims, with exasperation, "I know who you are!" I'm sure she does, but I still don't leave it to chance. Name confusion has prime embarrassment potential.

One time I was working at Folk City (a now-closed club in Greenwich Village). I was exhausted, and my brain wasn't working any too well. During my sound check a familiar-looking face came into the room. When I got through, I approached the person and introduced myself. He identified himself as Jackson Browne. At the time, I had not met Jackson, and the resemblance, combined with my fatigue, made the introduction plausible. I was taken in by the charade for probably thirty minutes. When the truth came out, I felt foolish and embarrassed. The person told other people about my confusion, and it left me with much bad feeling. (The person was, by the way, a fairly well-known singer in the pop folk vein.) It also created in me a strong commitment to avoid embarrassing other people whenever possible.

Please remember: Embarrassment is an invitation for deep resentment.

This is why it is so important not to admonish people in a loud, public voice. If your criticism is inappropriate, you'll be the fool. Yet even when it's accurate, if others can hear the criticism, you run the risk of embarrassing the person you're trying to correct. Any improvement in behavior will be mitigated by their resentment.

Before my show starts, I make a point of getting out of my dressing room and circulating through the crowd. (Given the atmosphere of most club dressing rooms, this is not a particularly difficult decision.) Out in the crowd, I shake hands, introduce myself, and smile. I feel like a politician and actually I am. I'm running for Top Ten.

I was in Japan a couple of years ago and my Japanese promoters were apoplectic when they found me mingling with the audience before my show. But the people in the audience were my employers. They had hired me by buying a ticket. I needed to see and touch them to make sure they were all right, to take in as much information as I could about the environment in which I was preparing to place my music.

No One Showed

Everyone knows what to do when you're playing to a sold-out crowd that thinks you're the greatest thing since shoe polish. But when the crowd is small, you and I are faced with three problems. First, the sadness at the size of the audience. Secondly, the financial reality that the promoter hasn't done very well. Lastly, the people in the audience, the fifteen or twenty people in the 150-seat club. They're worried. They're thinking, "Maybe I've made a mistake in coming to see Livingston. Maybe my taste isn't so good. Am I a chump for liking this guy?" Or, they're thinking, "Oh, how awful for him when I like him so much, and how hard it must be to play to so few of us." This is where show biz gets hard. Can I go onstage and face my sadness at the size of the audience and, at the same time, feel gratitude and love for the people who are there? Can I forgive myself for not drawing so well? Can I come up with a way to spread the financial loss around so the promoter will want to work with me again? You won't find these answers in Dave Mathews videos on MTV. Grace under pressure will dictate the length and quality of your career.

Get Comfy

It's important to stay within yourself when you perform. If the intent is to put the audience at ease, be sure to do material with which you are comfortable. Your career is not happening yesterday or tomorrow, but right now. The more time you spend in the past or the future, the less you'll have to spend in the present, which is your career.

BORIS: "Do you ever put yourself out on a limb with a song?"

Yes, but not far out. When I introduce a new song in my show, I just play bits of it at first and I open my eyes and ears and watch and feel. How is it going over? How do I feel when I am playing it? Can I sell it? Do I believe it? If I don't like the way it's going, I segue into something else. Because I work alone, I have this flexibility. If you are working in a larger production, your ability to change quickly is obviously reduced. However, you can and must be able to change as situations warrant.

KATHY: "How long does it take you to learn a song or a routine?"

For me, it can take years to learn a song because it goes beyond learning the words and music. It's learning the song so well that I can quickly adjust, twist, or shade it to the demands of a specific audience.

JASON: "I do a lot of cover songs [songs written by other people]. When I do my own songs, I like to tell people about them."

If that works for you, it's fine, but I usually avoid doing that. If the song doesn't move people, who cares where it came from? I've never heard anybody ask about a song they didn't like. If the song has moved them, they will find out about it.

I also avoid telling people what a song is about. Early on, when asked, I used to tell people what I had in mind when I wrote a song. I found that my reality invariably underwhelmed them. Today, if someone asks me what a song means, I turn the question back to them: "What do you think it means?" After they've told me their fantasy, I say, "Wow! That's amazing. That's just what I had in mind." They are delighted.

Please remember: The reality of your song is never as exciting as the audience's fantasy. A really good song has something different for everybody.

As we move into the performance part of this class, Trevor reads a poem by Edgar Allan Poe. I have him reread the last half. As he does, I turn off a fan that I left running in the back of the room.

"Do you hear the difference it makes to have that fan turned off?" (It's a rhetorical question . . . it makes a big difference.)

White noise (that is, the sound of air-handling or refrigeration units) is destructive to a show, and deadly for a performer.

White noise limits our dynamic range. White noise masks casual conversation, and worst of all, white noise makes it impossible to hear the subtle noises an audience uses to communicate with the performer.

The creaking chair, the crossing of legs, the cough—they're the sounds of someone who's bored shifting in his or her seat. These are very soft sounds. Some audiences are far more emphatic: "Yo, broccoli face! Get off the stage!" But generally, the signs of an unhappy audience are fairly quiet. White noise makes you deaf to the quiet grumbles of discontent. If the bright lights have already taken away your eyes, you are going to need your ears. When I go into a club or concert hall, I pay serious attention to white noise and eliminate it whenever I can.

The sounds of cash registers, blenders, and other human-operated noise generators in a club are invasive, but intermittent, and therefore not as corrosive as the steady hum of an air conditioner or refrigeration unit. I generally ask the "powers that be" (theater managers, club owners) to turn off any air-handling units when I am onstage. Be warned: They often balk, so when it comes to putting up with white noise or getting paid, go ahead and compromise. Don't let principles burn you alive. Live to fight another day!

Most amazing to me are the sound companies that set up amplifiers onstage with cooling fans that sound like coffee grinders. These people are hired to reinforce sound. Instead, they pollute the environment with their own white noise. Go figure.

I often play brand-new, expensive theaters where the designers have paid surprisingly little attention to their air-handling systems and have fatally polluted their theaters with white noise. In spite of the millions spent, they will never be good places to give or receive a performance. So sad. There is a lovely theater out on Long Island that renovated its air-handling equipment. When the job was done, the new equipment was so loud that the theater was ruined.

Air-handling equipment must be large enough to handle volume without velocity. Theater designers, if you're reading this, I beg you not to destroy a multimillion-dollar facility to save a few thousand on a ventilation system. The fancy sound system won't bail you out. Increased amplification will never compensate for lost silence.

Unfortunately, few people are familiar with true silence. They move from a raucous home to a noisy dorm, and live a life that includes a big family and a hard job in a noisy place. They rarely experience silence. When they do, it scares them. If you, as a performer, are comfortable with stillness and silence, you will be able to lead your audience through this unfamiliar environment. And, my friends, there is nothing more wonderful than complete silence in a sold-out hall—the anticipation of the paint on canvas.

Please remember: Silence is the canvas on which we paint our performance.

PHIL: "In the places that I play, the audience cheers for the baseball game on the TV. How do you compete with noise like that?"

This isn't a competition, Phil. We're not here to grab an audience away from something else. We're here to make sure they're doing okay. It's sad if they can get more entertainment from a TV screen than from us, but it's okay. They're the boss. It's their choice to make. I want an audience to have a good time no matter where it comes from. I bide my time and watch. I like to be ready for them when they're ready for me. It's important to me on many levels that I'm ready. However, being ready doesn't mean you're going to be called.

Please remember: It's sad to be ready and not be called. It's *tragic* to be called and not be ready.

There is always an ebb and flow to an audience and a show. Sometimes you have to let them go, wait your turn, and then reel them back in. Be patient. Ask yourself, "Where can I add to their enjoyment?" If they need to make noise, you might try getting quiet. If they can entertain themselves, let them. It's better when an audience comes to you out of attraction and need rather than trickery and gimmickry.

An analogy I like to use is that of somebody spearfishing. Thwack. The fish is speared and hauled in close. There's only one problem. Although it's close to you, it is either mortally injured or dead. That's okay if you're hungry, but hardly helpful if you're looking for a long-term relationship. We want to base our relationship with an audience on mutual attraction, not spear and retrieve.

Again, be patient and take your time. The hardest thing to realize as a performer is how much time you have. Where is the audience going to go? The answer is, nowhere, unless you *drive them away.* As I've said before, this is a big game of Simon Says. The audience has hired you to take control. They want to enter your reality. If you are still, they are still. If you are tense, they are tense. If you are at ease, they are at ease. If they trust you, they will put themselves in your hands.

Why do bands so often go onstage and yell, "Hey! How's everybody doing tonight?" Do you get the feeling that they actually care how the audience is doing? When someone yells, "How are you doing?" they are really saying, "I'm panicked. Please tell me how *I'm* doing." The audience crosses its collective arms and says (usually nonverbally), "Why don't you open your eyes and see how I am doing? Don't take my money and then force me to tell you how to take care of me."

Everything you do onstage tells a story about who you are and how you feel. You cannot hide. If you try to hide, you look like you're hiding. That tells a story, too.

At this point Jennifer, an earnest brunette from Tucson, comes onstage to read a short prose piece. Although she's fairly thin and small, Jennifer displays a stillness and sense of purpose that demand attention. When she gets to the end, before there is any applause, she says, "Thank you."

I question the timing and placement of the thank-you. After an audience applauds, it's fine to thank them. However, too often people use "thank you" as a signal that their performance is over. There is an easier, clearer way to show an audience that you are through. When you get to the end, be still and take in the effects of what you have put out. Finally, take a *slight bow.* A bow breaks the spell. It is the universally understood signal that a segment or the entire performance is over. Then, if they applaud, it's fine to thank them for their gift.

In your early career, when people are unfamiliar with your music, they need to be told when the end is at hand. If you neglect to tell them, they won't know. Have you ever felt the insecurity of not knowing whether an unfamiliar piece was over? Worse than that, have you ever applauded loudly at the wrong time? Most embarrassing. Don't ever leave an audience uninformed. Let them know when it's time to respond.

Krystal, a tall, statuesque African American, is the next person to perform. She has had professional modeling experience, so her presence onstage is quite arresting. She asks, "Livingston, do I have to have my piece memorized?"

Not necessarily. Let's see what happens if you read the piece instead of memorizing it. Krystal does this and it sounds fine, but there's one problem. When you read what you perform, your eyes are on the paper and not on them. As a result, your attention is diverted from the audience. So, it's fine to read, if you must, but I believe that audiences are paying you to pay attention to them. Anything that takes your attention from them is going to cost you.

At this point, in thinking about attention, I can't help but reflect on Krystal's appearance. The problem with being incredibly attractive is that people's attention and interest in you as a performer may never go beyond looks. They may never see what's on the inside, having set in concrete a fantasy based on the outside.

Kathy, who has a sweet, girl-next-door country western vibe, is the next to perform. As she speaks, her Texas accent soothes and amuses the class. She does a very nice job, but she also does something very common to newcomers on stage. She wiggles. She is in constant motion—I guess the theory being that a moving target is hard to hit.

Remember, as I've said before, performance is a big game of Simon Says. People suspend their reality and enter yours. Periodically, you have to be still or you will exhaust your audience. You must allow them places to rest and regroup, and they can do that only if *you* rest and regroup.

There is a big difference between being still and being rigid. [At this time, we all do an exercise of leaning forward and back, allowing our arms to be totally relaxed and to swing and fall at will.]

"It makes you all laugh to see me go forward and back with relaxed arms, doesn't it?" Relaxed arms are funny. They tell an audience that you are at ease. When you go from relaxed to being tense, it creates contrast, and that is good. Tense to tense? No contrast. Boring.

Arms are a great indicator of comfort. Loose arms are relaxing and funny to an audience. Mary Tyler Moore and Steve Martin or Richard Hunt who played Grover on *Sesame Street* are very good at this. Some people are so comfortable onstage that you will buy any plot they are selling. Bill Murray and the late Jim Hensen come to mind. They are so relaxed and at ease that no matter how ridiculous the premise, you will bite. Their total comfort is irresistible. You will willingly enter their reality. This is a great gift.

Why Would Anybody Want to Go Onstage?

People who are well adjusted and secure don't normally turn to the performing arts as a career choice. Lawyers, teachers, engineers, plumbers, and homemakers are the career choices of the better adjusted. Being in the performing arts is so difficult that if you didn't have to do it, you probably wouldn't.

Sometimes a lawyer or a doctor will approach me and express their desire to be onstage. I'm bemused by their naïveté. They don't understand that people who write, paint, dance, or sing do so not because they want to (in spite of what they tell themselves) but because they must. Nothing else seems to fit.

You want to be a performer even though you know there are easier career paths to choose, like the steady work and health care benefits found in a big corporation. Instead you're willing to go it alone in the cold, dimly lit world of the performing arts. You didn't choose to be here. Nobody does. You are here because you're driven. As a group, we performers tend to be insecure and rather hard on ourselves—demanding more of ourselves than we can reasonably deliver. These are states of mind that can cause us big trouble. They make us nervous and fearful, driving away the very audience we so badly need. At this point I need to descend into some psychobabble, and I want to apologize in advance.

I see most life situations as falling into four distinct steps. Using the familiar environment of driving a car, let's go through them.

ONE: ACTION. You're driving along the highway, and out of the blue, somebody cuts you off. It was unexpected and it scares the bejesus out of you. The fear triggers a huge adrenaline rush, which throws you into state number two.

TWO: REACTION. Words are spoken, harsh stares exchanged, predictable hand signals given. Adrenaline, fear, and rage are in full swing. This is a *very dangerous* place to be. Events are accelerating and can easily move out of control. This is when people say and do things they often later regret. As time passes, you start to calm down and you move to the third state.

THREE: ACCEPTANCE. Another word for *acceptance* is *sadness,* or the heartbreak of the hand you've been dealt, the unfairness of life. "I'm just driving along, minding my own business, and this maniac cuts me off. I could have wrecked my car. I could have been killed. What kind of world are we living in? People are turning into terrible drivers. What a crummy day." Although painful, this state of acceptance is actually quite safe. Sadness has replaced panic, and it is the sadness of acceptance that allows us to reach the fourth place, one where the most attractive of human qualities dwells.

FOUR: FORGIVENESS. "We're both okay. I've driven that way myself sometimes. I've been out of control in the past, and others have cut me slack." Have you ever looked in your rearview mirror after inadvertently cutting someone off? After the initial surprise, you cringe in anticipation of the expected rage. You screw up your courage and glance in the mirror again, and when the person you've almost hit shakes their head, visibly sighs and looks slightly away, it's clear that they're letting your trespass slide. You are forgiven. The total relief that comes from being forgiven, or for forgiving others, allows life to move on.

Let's see how these four steps relate to being onstage when the circumstances you find yourself in do not fit your preconceived fantasy.

ONE: ACTION. I walk onstage and the environment bears no resemblance to my expectation.

TWO: REACTION. In the unexpected, unfamiliar environment, panic, nervousness, and fear overwhelm me, and I become completely self-centered. Will I remember my lyrics? Will I pass out? Will I make a fool of myself? Am I going to throw up? I am devastated by falling so short of my lofty expectations.

THREE: ACCEPTANCE. After the performance I eventually accept the reality of what happened. The experience wasn't what I expected or hoped for. I was not good. I might even have been the worst I can possibly be—absolutely awful. I desperately wanted to be good and I must accept the fact that I simply was not. I am so sad and my heart is broken.

FOUR: FORGIVENESS. I did the best I could with what I had. I accept responsibility for what happened, and for the audience's decision about me.

When I am nervous, it's a signal to me that I am fearful and out of control, that I am in the dangerous reactive state. What am I scared of? Being awful. Being embarrassed. Making a fool of myself. Instead of staying in this dangerous place, I simply move ahead. I allow myself to feel the total heartbreak that I would feel if my fears came true, if I were truly "absolutely awful" onstage.

We've already discussed the fact that audiences do not want your fear or bitterness. They have plenty of their own. The question is, will they accept your sadness? The answer: an unequivocal yes. Audiences *love* sadness and contrition. (Therein the success of virtually all country music.) And self-forgiveness? That they love that, goes without saying.

It's okay to be human onstage, to forget lyrics, to sing wrong notes. Not only do audiences forgive your humanness, they love it. They love you to be normal, to make a mistake, acknowledge it, smile, shake your head slightly, forgive yourself, and move on.

The ability to forgive is very attractive. When an audience sees that you can forgive yourself, they make the assumption (probably correctly) that you will *forgive them, too.* That makes them comfortable, and comfortable audiences gladly pay your salary.

Jason, a shy northern Ohio native, walks onstage, introduces himself, and gives a short explanation of what he's about to do. There's a problem. Everything he says sounds like a question.

When each? phrase you speak? sounds like a question? it forces an audience? into a state of tension? and *drives them crazy.* They want to be told, not asked; informed, not quizzed.

People turn sentences into questions because they're insecure. They need constant affirmation that the audience is supporting them. Audiences are normally filled with good, decent people who, if asked to, will give that affirmation to the person onstage. But if they've received nothing before they are asked to give, it turns the giving process into a one-sided chore.

The performances in class continue with poetry and prose readings. Some students have a natural charisma, others virtually none. Although charisma and looks provide a slight advantage when you first step onstage, they, like "talent," are vastly overrated. Because, again, the quality of performance is contingent on what you can *take in,* not what you put out.

As noted before, the key to your success lies in making your audience comfortable. Of course, you hope for the best to happen, but if the worst should happen—if you are absolutely awful—you are fully capable of accepting the audience's judgment; and, although your heart is broken, you are also capable of forgiving them and yourself. Of course, it's easier to say than to do. Trust me, I'm still working on it. Wish me luck.

ALL THINGS
IN GOOD TIME

I have a question for the class. Who is the leader of the band?

Boris answers, "Lead singer." Lee is convinced it's the arranger. Charlotte says it's the person doing the solo.

"Nice thoughts, people. Nice but wrong." The leader of the band is the person who holds the time, the person who has the *best rhythm.*

The person with the best rhythm is the person to whom you return to get your bearings, to settle down, to reconnect.

Rhythm and time are the elements that allow you to be hypnotized. Tick tock. Tick tock. Tick tock. You are under my spell. A strong, even rhythm tells an audience that you are in control. That they can safely abandon their reality and enter yours.

Once you've committed your performance to predictable time, you cannot break it. If, for whatever reason, you have "timus interruptus," you are in big trouble. Interrupting time is the signature of panic. More than anything else you say or do, interrupting time tells an audience "I am out of control. I don't know what I'm doing. This ship may be going down." Their response will be to leave your reality and reenter their own—to swim for their lives.

Rhythm is the foundation on which we build our performance. One, two, three, four. One, two, three, four. One, two, three, four. Strong, even, confident. Time predicts the future. After three beats that are strong and even, all successive beats are predictable to *infinity*. The audience feels this and surrenders completely. For proof, I offer you Ray Charles. Listening to Ray Charles is like falling into a featherbed. His time is so perfect, so confident, so dependable that after the required three beats you are totally enveloped and free to let go completely. "Yo, Ray, you drive." (By the way, there is a young singer named Marty Sexton with a similar talent.)

Good time speaks for itself. Let's talk about bad time and what makes it that way.

I say to Phil, do me a favor and snap your fingers. (Phil starts snapping.) That's right. 1-2-3-4. 1-2-3-4. 1-2-3-4. 1-2-3-4, right on the beat. Now keep it up. (Forty seconds pass.) How is Phil doing? He's falling apart, isn't he? Why? Why is the time falling apart? It's crumbling because his fingers are getting tired. The lactic acid is building up and the muscles are starting to burn. They ache. They cry for relief. They demand complete attention. He forgets the crowd. He forgets the music. He forgets his responsibilities. The pain must be addressed. And, in spite of his best efforts, the time falls apart.

You cannot hold rhythm externally. It must be internalized. Once the time is inside you, you can give it to any part of your body that you want. Sometimes you sway or tap your right foot and then your left. Maybe you turn your head or push a shoulder forward and back. If the time comes from within, it will show up on the most-rested, comfortable outside part; hand, foot, eyes, hip, head, they all trade off. As one part becomes tired, another takes over. Watch people sway at Carnival. Watch a Zulu or Native

American dancer. Their time is internalized, effortless, and completely joyous. They can keep it up for hours. People, this is going to be coming soon to a body near you.

If you are in time and at ease, the audience stays put. They are yours. The only way you'll drive them away is by being in a state of tension and fear. So find a way to be comfortable. Now, I can read your minds and I know you're thinking, "I don't need to keep time; that's what the drummer's there for." Has anybody here ever played with a drummer who couldn't keep time? All hands rise. Never abdicate time to the drummer or a piano player. It is everyone's job to hold and internalize rhythm. It's wonderful to immerse yourself in a blistering guitar solo or vocal "emote" and then, when you come back to earth from your journey, there are your band mates, welcoming you back with the strong, even rhythm they've been keeping in your absence.

The conductor holds the baton. Watch the tip. Up, down, side, side. Up, down, side, side. One, two, three, four. The change in the baton's direction represents the moment in time that is the beat.

At a distance, the baton looks fairly sharp. The time seems pretty good. But up close, under a magnifying glass, the point of the direction change may get ragged and dull. It may be early or late. A little loud, or a bit tentative.

Please remember: There is a precise moment in time that is the beat. The more focused you are on that instant, the more sharply you can bring the beat into focus. More focus means higher intensity.

What do you do during all the time that is *not* the beat? The greatest benefit of sharpening your rhythmic focus is that during all the space that is not the beat, *you can rest*. You can prepare yourself for that next moment in time. That next beat. This drives audiences wild. Remember Simon Says. They'll be resting with you. Often, they will be ready for the next beat before it's time. But you are in control and will not be rushed. The beat will be delivered when necessary, but not an instant before. When it is finally delivered, the audience will be completely receptive and most grateful.

One of the best examples I know of this "focus-and-rest" concept is drummer Russ Kunkel. His focus is so sharp that the listener is hypnotized by the anticipation of the next beat. To paraphrase the wine commercial, "Russ Kunkel will serve no beat before its time." You must rest. You must have time to be still and renew yourself. If you don't rest, you cannot sustain the energy. You will become strained and fall apart. For self-protection, the audience will tune out and turn away.

So, again, how do you hold attention and rest at the same time? By focusing on the instant in time that is the beat. The greater the focus, the more time to rest. The more you rest, the more comfortable you are. The more comfortable you are, the more comfortable the audience will be. And we know what comfortable audiences will do.

I have a core within me that is the beat, and I send that beat to different parts of me: feet, fingers, hands, face, shoulders, hips, belly.

A great way of learning how to internalize time is to march. I love marching. It is God's way of enabling high school kids from Iowa to internalize time. Find a grove and live in it. Tick tock. Tick tock. Tick tock.

It's amazing the external things people depend upon to maintain rhythm. A metronome, the drunken enthusiasm of a bar crowd, or most commonly, rhythm dictated by panic are good examples. How fast can I play? Get those fingers to top speed and that is the time. Please do not depend on a metronome or other externals for time. A metronome is like life support. Though occasionally very handy, it is not conducive to a flexible lifestyle.

Again, time must come from the inside. Practice internalizing time. Try this: Count off. As you walk down the street, count your steps in groups of four. Hum a simple melody that's in time with your steps. Try this, too: Tap out syncopation against a predictable rhythm source—windshield wipers, turn signals, a washing machine out of balance, a blinking yellow light, anything that is repetitious. Only after you become fully comfortable, after the time is established, then and *only then,* can you start to place notes, chords, melody, and lyric. The foundation must be strong for the house to stand.

Once you've established your rhythm, look at your audience. How are they doing? How do they feel?

ARNOLD asks: "Livingston, what are we looking for? I feel sort of stupid just staring at a crowd."

Arnold, you're not staring, you're looking for people who want to have a conversation with you. A smile, a nod, a slight move that tells you what they're feeling. The music, lyrics, and rhythm are the conduit through which the non-verbal communication goes back and forth.

Now that you've got your rhythm established, go ahead and dance a little dance. You heard me. *Dance.* People may laugh. If you dance like me, they definitely will. Don't worry. Laugh with them. Let them see that you can forgive yourself for being goofy. The attempt can bring great pleasure. Clearly, Berry Gordy of Motown Records understood that a little choreography and dance paid huge performance dividends. If I had my way, all performers would be in dance class for at least half of each and every day.

Please remember: A performer in a dance class is a performer interested in success.

Play the Hand You're Dealt

Boris is the day's first performer. He's a curious, outgoing twenty-two-year-old from a suburb of Munich, Germany. Clear-eyed and friendly, he tackles Otis Redding's "Dock of the Bay" a capella. At the end of his performance, I ask, "How was the time in the bridge?"

"It fell apart," says Trevor.

"Why? Where was the concentration of the time?"

"In his foot."

"And the foot got tired and the time fell apart. Please bring time into your core and then send it into various parts of your body. If the left foot gets tired, give it to the right foot."

Next up: Phil, a tall, outgoing twenty-six-year-old from a Boston suburb. A worried look is fixed on his face, and when he gets onstage and sings an a capella piece, he complains about not having a guitar to accompany him.

Phil, I sympathize with your situation, but what can I do? Someone had to go first, and I won't let anyone accompany themselves yet. I'm sorry about the hand you were dealt. Let me tell you about the hand that was dealt to me this past weekend. On Friday night, I played at Regis College in a Boston suburb. On Saturday, I flew to Washington, D.C., for two shows in a small club. I went to bed at 2:30 A.M. and woke up at 5:30 A.M. to fly home to Boston. Sunday morning, I attended a memorial service for my grandmother. That evening, in Concord, Massachusetts, I performed at a free outdoor concert with various other artists. By the time I hit that stage, I was fried. My brain was molasses. I knew that it was going to be a struggle to see or hear my audience clearly. However, I refused to compound my difficulties by beating myself up for not being a hundred percent. My responsibility was to monitor myself, take stock of what I had left, and do my best.

I didn't play very well. I wasn't spontaneous. The cobwebs of fatigue didn't allow me to be nimble enough to respond to the moment. It was very frustrating.

People came up to me afterward and said, "Livingston, you were great!"

I looked them in the eye, shook their hands, and said, "Thank you. I had a terrific time, too."

It was a lie. I didn't belong there. I belonged in bed or at least on a couch with a channel surfer.

But what gives me the right to dispute or to take someone else's pleasure at anything other than face value? A compliment is a gift, and graciously receiving a gift is a very kind act. You do the monitoring. Let God do the judging.

Hecklers

If you're dealing with audiences in any kind of meaningful way, you're going to have to deal with hecklers. First off, let's define a heckler. It's somebody who is steadily and aggressively disruptive. They can be that way for three reasons: (1) they are angry, agitated, and uncomfortable, and need to express it; (2) they are mentally unstable and unable to judge the disruptiveness of their state; or (3)— the most usual—they are chemically blasted and oblivious to their reduced capacity for reasonable social intercourse.

If you're watching the space where you'll be playing before you go onstage, it's pretty easy to spot a group that will be disruptive, particularly if they're drunk. Be aware, but don't react too early. Let other audience members work on them first. Group pressure solves nine out of ten cases of boorish behavior.

If they're oblivious to group pressure, then eventually you've got to step in. After two or three concerned, serious looks in their direction, the first words I say are, "Guys, I'm not going to be here much longer. When I'm done, it'll be your turn." I generally say that off mike and directly to them. Again, in most cases, that's enough to solve the problem. However, once in a great while (every two or three years), I'm faced with someone who is so disruptive that I have to speak with them directly. I'll break rhythm, still my guitar strings, and say on mike to the audience, "Excuse me for a moment." I'll then either put down my guitar or not, depending on where they're located, and I'll walk over to the disruptive person. I go directly to them because we need to have a private discussion. What I'm going to say is so strong that I don't want any more of the audience than is necessary to hear it.

Let me tell you, it's bad news to have the person who was onstage a moment ago walking in your direction with a deep frown on his face.

I crouch beside the person, make sure I have their attention (not always easy), and say, "Your behavior is enormously disruptive and I need it to stop. If it does not stop, I'm not going to continue to play. Do you understand?" I stay with them until I'm convinced they understand, then I return to the stage. As yet, I have not ever had to leave a show prematurely with the exception of the aforementioned Jethro Tull incident.

Most audience troubles occur late at night. Many hours of drinking make for some interesting situations. A few nights ago I was playing a second show in a Chinese restaurant next to a tattoo parlor on Main Street in Woonsocket, Rhode Island. (I, too, have to take what work I can.)

I noticed before the show that there was a raucous table of eight or so people just to my right. Sure enough, when I started to play, they started acting up. The show was sold out, and I was under substantial pressure from the rest of the audience to stop this disruption. They, too, had paid their money and wanted to enjoy my show without the drunken intrusions.

"I wanta sing. I wanta sing something," one particularly blasted member of this group kept saying. I was inclined to let him try, but I had a problem. If I let him onstage and didn't control the situation, he might become a clown for his group—bringing them along and putting me fully out of control of the show. I kept cool until a plan occurred to me. I played a song called "On and On," by Stephen Bishop. During the bridge of the song, the melody goes up to a high A. Before I sang the line preceding the note, I looked over at the guy and said, "You want to sing something, don't you?"

"Yeah."

"Then come up here, right now, and sing this one note. Do you think you can handle that?" Predictably, over-estimating his ability, he stumbled up onstage and I set the trap. I sang, "Hold on tight, don't let her say good night." As the melody rose to that high A note, I left it for him. Nothing. Of course, he missed it completely. At that point, I turned to the audience and repeated the same line. At the appropriate moment, they seized the opportunity to high-light this guy's incompetence and sang the note clear, loud, and strong. I instructed the intoxicated would-be singer to sit down. He did and was not heard from again. Frankly, I was a bit lucky. My plans do not always work out so well.

Okay, let's perform.

Krystal sings a spiritual. She gets to the end of a fine performance and a pained expression crosses her face.

I ask the class: "What about that last face?"

KRYSTAL interjects: "I messed up."
JASON counters: "We don't know this song. Unless you tell us, we don't know that you've made a mistake."

Even if we did know the song, we don't mind a mistake. We're all human, and humans make mistakes. We forgive you, no harm, no foul. But, if you don't forgive yourself, if a small mistake is occasion for a pained expression, how is the audience supposed to feel? It tells them that you beat up on yourself for small things. If you can't forgive yourself for a small human mistake, how will you treat a very human audience? It makes them wonder. It makes them worry. "If she beats up on herself, yipes, what's she going to do to me?" Once again, self-acceptance and forgiveness are attractive qualities onstage. Sadly, they require a great deal of work.

Charlotte sings a Nanci Griffith song a capella. Charlotte is from San Francisco. Attractively prim, she is firm in her belief that hard work and fairness will triumph. I hope she's right. When she's finished, she asks, "During an earlier class you said that when we're onstage, our job is to take in and make adjustments. Should we also try to build these spaces into our rehearsal times?"

I don't think so, because you never know what's going to happen onstage until you're there. What you want to do in rehearsal is to learn the content of your performance (songs, words, notes) well enough so when you are onstage you can concentrate less on the content and more on what's happening around you. You can make your performance become part of the fabric of the moment. You rehearse so the performance is automatic and you are free to be completely neutral onstage, free to observe, process, and react.

I ask the class, Who has had a wonderful rehearsal only to have the performance turn into a nightmare? (All hands go up.) You play well in your room at night and then—ka-pow!—you're onstage being blindsided by events beyond your control. The playing field has changed.

Please remember: The rehearsal is no closer than a second cousin to the performance—a distant relation at best.

Ride, Arnie, Ride

Arnold, do a little mental exercise for me. What street are we on?

ARNOLD: *"Boylston."*

I want you to mentally get on a bicycle and start peddling down Boylston Street. Comfy?

"Yeah."

Cruising along.

"Yeah!"

Now you're approaching the intersection of Boylston and Arlington Street. What are you going to do?

ARNOLD: *"Uuh, stop?"*

What if the light is green?

ARNOLD: *"Uuh, go?"*

What you're telling me is you don't know what you're going to do at the intersection because you're not there yet. Right? Are you worried?

"Nope."

Of course not. You've ridden a bicycle for years, and when you get to the intersection, you'll make the appropriate decision. But it's impossible to plan in advance because you're not yet there.

Again, after thirty-odd years and four thousand–plus shows, the one thing I've learned for certain is that I have *no* ability to predict the course of a show until I get onstage. Everybody around me knows what is going to hap-

51

pen. Wife, friends, managers, and family will all have an opinion for me. They are invariably wrong. Show up neutral. Take in, then react. Enjoy the process as it unfolds.

The Bat

The very best argument for performing with restraint, reserve, and a neutral attitude is that it allows you to handle the unexpected. And when onstage, the unexpected *will* happen. It is the unexpected and unique that are the source of the most vivid performance memories for both performer and audience.

A case in point: I was working the second show in Geddis' Pub in Bar Harbor, Maine. The crowd was pumped, the joint was full, and the weather was uncharacteristically warm. The windows were open wide, and the touch of breeze this allowed felt great. Halfway through the show, a small and, doubtless, very surprised bat flew right through one of those windows. It was bedlam. Females with visions of having a rabid bat irrevocably tangled in their hair hit the floor with a scream. Males whose macho fantasies were colliding head on with memories of old cheap horror movies joined them. The bat—not at all understanding the sea of confusion that greeted his innocent search for bugs—zoomed around the room in circles.

As for me, I love bats. Wife and dog aside, it's maybe my favorite mammal; in this case, an innocent, industrious creature clearly involved with the wrong crowd. So here's the scene. All these people huddled on or near the floor, eyes glued to this circling, panicked creature. I concocted a plan. I instructed the people on the right side of the room to, on my say-so, wave their hands and arms. When the bat circled to the left, I gave the word. Their hands waved, and the bat's circle became smaller. Progressively, toward the left, more and more people waved their hands and stood their ground. When finally confronted with no more room to circle, the bat took the remaining option and departed the way it had come. The resulting cheer was both heartfelt and enthusiastic, and when the next song in the set was an abbreviated version of the *Batman* TV theme, a good laugh was had by all.

Next to perform is Dustin, a quiet, thoughtful young man with thick glasses that hide slightly sad eyes. He plays a challenging classical piece on his guitar.

How did he do?

ARNOLD: "Well, he did very nicely, but he spent all his time watching his guitar. He didn't look around very much."

This is a dilemma. You want to stay in your instrument and concentrate on the nuances and subtleties of your performance. By the same token, you want to take in as much as possible of what is going on around you. If you cannot do two things at once, you need to prioritize. There is a solution.

Let's go back to Dustin. "Dustin, play a simple blues."

He begins to play.

How is the rhythm? Is it better than before?

Most say yes.

How about his eye contact with the audience? Does he seem as nervous?

Kathy responds, "His eye contact is better. He's much more at ease."

In short, Dustin's second performance was far better than the first. He simplified things. He played a piece that was under his control. As a result, he had the time and space to check on his surroundings. He was more comfortable and more pleasant to be around.

If you carry music onstage with technical demands that monopolize your energy, you're asking for trouble. In the rehearsal hall, dorm room, or next-door neighbor's garage, it all fits together so well. But throw in the complications of the onstage environment and you have a recipe to crash and burn.

Instrumentalists seem to stay more within their instruments than singers do. Miles Davis comes to mind. However, think about Louis Armstrong or Kenny G. They always give the impression that they are plugged into the moment. They are aware of the audience around them. As a result, the audience feels they are able to communicate with the performer, to make a difference in the course of events, empowered and happy.

Jennifer performs "My Heart Belongs to Me." She does a fine job. Great focus and stillness at the end of the song. We are transfixed. She's chosen a good song and performed it well. I suggest that hand movements and gestures would help to illustrate the lyrics. She balks.

"I never use my hands in normal conversation."

"Oh, really? Do me a favor. Help me with a skit."

I pretend to be a meter person writing out a fifty-dollar ticket when her car is parked in a completely legal space.

Jennifer gets into the swing of the skit and articulates justifiable outrage at the situation's unfairness. The class is amused to see her arms flailing wildly as she protests the injustice of the undeserved ticket.

You use your hands, arms, and body in everyday life much more than you think. So when you *don't* use them onstage, it's unnatural and noticeable. The lesson being, use your arms, use your hands, use everything you've got at your disposal. If you don't have to hold an instrument, use that freedom to shape with your hands what is going on in the lyrics. No microphone keeping you in one place? Use the freedom to move around.

What do you have to work with? In the early parts of your career, not many externals. Don't despair. There's plenty on the inside. A brain to evenly and accurately process input from all the senses. Cleanly disciplined rhythm to hypnotize the audience and allow the sensory input to be shared. And the resiliency of youth that allows you to take a licking and keep on ticking. (To take a thumping and keep on bumping. To take a whipping and keep on tripping. Your choice.)

REALITY

An audience comes to see your performance. They suspend their world and enter yours, the tick tock of your rhythm, the flow of pictures painted with lyrics, notes and chords on the jet black canvas of silence. That's the ideal. Let's get back to reality.

Here's a quiz for you: What's the difference between a preacher and an entertainer? Beep. Time's up.

A preacher gets paid on the *way out*. An entertainer gets paid on the *way in*. If you've taken their money, you are an entertainer. You have been hired to pay attention to them. Do your job.

I ask the class about the clubs they have been able to play in.

Club Jabberwock at Syracuse.
The Tam in Boston.
The Knees in Worcester.

How was the Knees?

LAURA: "It was a scary rat hole."

Woah. That's pretty graphic. How was the sound? "Pretty crappy." The lights? "Almost nonexistent." Why didn't you ask for better? "I guess we didn't deserve it." No, no, no! I won't hear that. Of course, you deserve it. True, you're not going to get it, but you do deserve it. You are conscientious students, good sons and daughters, fine friends. You deserve the best. But you're still not going to get it. Why?

"The club owner is greedy and doesn't want to spend the money."

Perhaps, but that's not why you can't get what you want. As I've said before, how good is your power base? At this point in your career, how many people can you draw into a club?

Not many. Long faces indicate the class understands this reality.

The truth is, because you cannot yet draw a large audience, you cannot generate enough income to make demands of a club owner. So you are going to have to make do with what is there.

I worked at a club called The Iron Horse in Northampton, Massachusetts, a few months ago. I arrived at the club around four for a five o'clock sound check. When I went downstairs to go to the bathroom I found it was pretty funky. So guess what I did? I cleaned it.

"Ugh! Harsh!" says Kathy.

No, it was fine. I took some paper towels out of the trash and used them to scrub down the sink and toilet. After I straightened up the bathroom, I cleaned up the trash and cigarette butts around the club's entrance, then scrubbed down. Obviously, I wish the club staff had done these things, but they didn't. Maybe they were too busy or they just didn't see it (like the mess in my music room). For whatever reason, it wasn't a priority. If I beat on the staff about cleaning the club, they were just going to get resentful, and any improvement in appearance would be canceled by the mutinous mood of already overworked people performing extra duty. The ability to show up early and do the low and funky jobs speaks volumes about how seriously you take your performance.

Please remember: I don't clean toilets and pick up cigarette butts for the club owners. I do it for my audience. They buy the tickets and I work for them. In buying a ticket, they have hired me. They are my boss, and I don't like my boss having to stand in line looking at cigarette butts or using dirty bathrooms. Do they know I've done these things? I hope not.

When I am working in a club, I expect that place to come up to my standards. I don't care to go down to its standards. Detail, detail, detail. Good careers are in the details.

You're Not Paranoid, They Are Watching You

Your concert starts not when you go onstage but the moment you show up at the job. People are watching you. Door people, waiters, bartenders, sound people.

How do you look when you show up for a performance? Is your van beat up? Are you beat up? Is your equipment all dirty and taped? Are your electronics filled with buzzes? You're sending encyclopedias of nonverbal signals about the type of person you are. By your actions, you show other people how you want them to behave.

If you make a bad impression on the club's staff, then they can make your show uncomfortable in the extreme. Show up early. Look and listen. Identify and, if you're very lucky, solve problems.

Opening Act

When I am the opening act for an artist who is billed above me, I like to keep in mind that, in the main, the audience is there to hear the lead act. I direct my attention to making the headliner look good. "Good evening. It is wonderful to be in Columbus tonight and to be sharing a stage with Bonnie Raitt. She is *so* fantastic. I'm going to play about twenty minutes and then I'm going to turn you over to her." If you are the opening act, *be quick* and *be good.* The better the opening act, the better it is for the headliner.

When I am the lead act, I love it when my opener is great because it reflects well on me. Sometimes I'll be sitting backstage listening to an audience go wild for the opening act. What's tough for my ego is good for my audience. If the opening act is terrific, be sure to acknowledge their quality. And if you can work it out, get them to come onstage with you. They're great, and you get the credit.

Keep in mind the same audience that thanks you for a good opening act will blame you for a bad one. It's grim to follow a terrible opening act. You step onstage and the audience's gaze tells you, "Ouch, that hurt. Why did you subject me to that?" A rotten opening act can test the good humor of the best of crowds.

When you're the opening act, even if you're doing very well, do not let the audience's enthusiasm keep you onstage too long. There's no better way to put yourself on the headliner's dirt list than to use up the enthusiasm of their crowd. *Know when to get off.*

If you're the opening act, make it your business to meet and discuss show length with the headliner. You'll find a remarkable disparity between how long the headliner wants you to play (six minutes) and the length of time the promoter or club owner wants you to play (two and a half hours). Find a compromise. In advance.

I've had a lot of interesting experiences with opening acts. One time I was working at a small theater in Sarasota, Florida. The front doors were made of thick glass that had gotten all smudgy. I arrived early and had some time to kill, so I got some Windex and began cleaning the doors. (My wife, Maggie, wonders why this skill miraculously vanishes the moment I get home.)

Enjoying the simple monotony of the task, I looked down the street and noticed a young woman with a guitar walking toward the theater. An entourage of three followed her, and all four of them, shoulders squared, were obviously filled with the hopeful career implications of being the opening act for Livingston Taylor.

As they came up the steps, I held the door for them. Staring straight ahead, they purposefully walked right past me. The reason they didn't recognize me was simple. Their fantasy of a headliner did not include a window washer. Livingston Taylor with Windex two hours before the show? Impossible. Trust me, it's possible.

How Good Can You Be?

Guys, how important is it to be good onstage? How important to play at the absolute top of your ability?

STUDENTS: Very important. The most important thing.

What if I were to tell you that the audience basically doesn't care? Let's make up an example. Say you go to see Fleetwood Mac with a woman you've been seeing for about a year. You're crazy about her, and your relationship has been growing closer and stronger. You want to move it to the next level. So while Stevie Nicks sings "Landslide," you lean close and whisper in your date's ear, "Sandy, I've loved our time together. I believe you are the most special person I have ever met. Will you marry me?"

With tears in her eyes, she kisses you softly and answers, "Yes."

Okay, how do you feel about the show? Yeah, pretty good. Did it matter that Stevie Nicks's voice might have been scratchy that night or that your seats weren't so great? That the sound had too much bass or the backup singer had a cold sore? No, of course not. In your memory the concert is one of the high points of your life.

Now suppose there's a couple at this same show for whom things have not been going well. During this same song, she turns to him and says, "Tom, I'm sorry, but this isn't working. I've tried but I can't get it back. We've moved in different directions, and I'm sorry to say there's nothing left. I'm all through. Tomorrow I'm going to pack my things and move out." How was the Fleetwood Mac concert for these two? Yeah, the worst. Forever in their memories, "Landslide" will remind them of one of the most painful moments in their life—regardless of how well the band played that night.

I ask the class, "Who here has been to a big show recently?"

Jason says, *"Billy Joel."*

"Where?"

"At the Fleet Center."

"Who did you go with?"

"Three friends."

"Did you go to dinner before the show?"

"Yeah."

"How far in advance did you make these plans?"

"About a month."

You built an entire evening around Billy Joel. But his concert was just one part of your evening—a crucial part, but hardly the whole night. So, if Billy Joel's voice was a little scratchy, or his piano a bit out of tune, it was okay. You still had a great time.

Nobody's asking you to be perfect. Nobody's asking you to be one hundred percent. But you are being asked to do the best you can with what you've got at the time. Does the audience care if you're tired or ill? Basically, no. They want to hear that you're glad to be in their presence, that they are the center of your attention. They will worry about you, if you ask them to, but they would much prefer that you worry about them.

Favorite Place to Play

"Livingston, where's your favorite place to play?" Arnold asks.

That, my struggling student, is simple. My favorite place to play is *always* where I'm playing. An audience member in some small town in some nondescript theater or club will approach me and invariably ask me, "Where's your favorite place to play?" I look them clean in the eye, smile, and say, "Right here. In Steubenville, Ohio. *This* is my favorite place to play in the whole wide world." They frown as they scour my face, looking for any hint of a lie. They won't find it because I have told the truth. Regardless, they don't look long because they would love to believe that where I am is where I want to be. They don't really want to know my favorite place. What they do want to know is where they rank on my list. They're hoping for a high ranking. When they find out they're number one, they're delighted. I work very hard to put myself in a frame of mind that allows me to believe that wherever I am is the place I most want to be.

Play live any chance you get. Only by playing in front of people and watching them do you gain the experience and knowledge about the parts of you that work well with a crowd.

Arnold asks if my "favorite place to play" includes benefits.

In all honesty, I'm not crazy about doing benefits. Often as not, everybody winds up unhappy. The benefit recipients usually don't get the amount of money they had in mind, the volunteer staff running the show is mostly inexperienced, and the audience basically resents having their affection for someone's performance used to support some outside cause they may or may not believe in. I think it's safer to work, make money, and give it quietly to the cause of your choice.

I think audiences instinctively know that when their money is going to you or your promoter, you have a vested interest in them having the best time they legally possibly can.

Avoid, at all costs, any political event. If the person gets elected and does something stupid (highly likely), your support of that person will be remembered and held against you. That said, I've found the pressures to resist benefits and political fund-raisers almost impossible and wind up doing lots of them. I wish you better luck.

Lighting

In the performance classroom at Berklee there is a small stage, a modest sound system, and a few lights. Boris stands on the stage and prepares to sing. Before he starts, we talk about lights. Good, well-focused lights in the hands of a competent lighting designer are an amazing asset to a show. However, the lights we're going to get in the clubs we start out in are not going to be good (if they exist at all). When in doubt, keep lights as bright as they will go and use plenty of clear or amber gels; don't wash yourself out with greens, blues, or purples. Bright white lights allow you to be seen.

BORIS: "But when you have bright lights in your eyes, doesn't that limit how much you can see, and how much contact you can have with your audience?"

Yes, it restricts your contact; however, bright lights do light up a portion of the audience as well, and you've still got your other senses to call on. My lighting rule is: Always use whatever lights you can. Keep them clear and bright. Bad lighting is still better than none.

Once, during a career lull in the mid-seventies, I was hired to play at a small college in Worcester, Massachusetts. In the room where they were having the concert, there were no lights at all. None. I asked a rather unenthusiastic student who was running the show if he had any thoughts about this oversight. He didn't. Because I had showed up early, I had time to run over to Kmart and buy three clip-on-type floodlights, three 100-watt bulbs to go in them, and an extension cord. I clipped them on the ceiling, and the problem was minimally solved.

Boris sings a pleasant ballad a capella. There are periods during his song when he marks time and waits for another lyric to begin. During these times he looks down at his feet. I say, "Boris, how are your feet doing? Are they enjoying your singing? Are they paying your salary?" You might think about taking a moment when you are not concentrating on your singing to look around and see what effect your music and presence are having on the people in your environment. Look, listen, feel, and think. Your job onstage is to take in, to have that nonverbal conversation we've talked about.

Kathy gets onstage and sings Patsy Cline's "Crazy." At the end, I ask, "How was that?" Someone remarks that the time was a little shaky. "Was she late in the time or did she rush?"

PHIL: "She rushed."

Think about that song. "I'm crazy 2-3-4 . . . Crazy for feeling so lonely 3-4-5-6-7-8 . . . Crazy . . ." That's a lot of space when you're singing a capella. With all that open space, Kathy got worried. She seemed to ask herself, "Maybe I should be doing something? Will they hang with me while I wait for the next lyric?" She panicked. And rushed.

Nothing tells an audience that you are ill at ease like rushing the beat. It says, "Get me to the next phrase and get me out of here." Please avoid indicating to your audience that you don't like being in their presence. Wait for the moment in time that is the beat with patience and dignity.

Sometimes the audience wants you to rush. A worked-up crowd in a bar is often guilty of this. In their passion to get higher, they will demand that the band rush. You must resist the temptation to fall into their euphoria. You are the "designated driver." Make them wait for the moment in time that is the beat. They will ultimately appreciate your discipline.

Please remember: Passion without discipline is yucky. An audience will never accept your passion unless they are held by your discipline.

Lee comes onstage and plays a simple piece with drumsticks on a chair. The playing is nice. Yet when he introduced himself, I couldn't hear his name. I ask him to repeat it. He swallows it again. Not good. People *must* hear your name. Tell it to them time and time again. Make sure people know who you are. If someone doesn't know who you are, how will they ever find you?

Lee looks down and is clearly worried about being on-stage. "Lee, you need to remember that when you're on-stage, you are not running a democracy. You're in charge, and people want you to be. Accept the fact that you're not going to please everybody. Heck, some nights you're not going to please anybody. But you have the right to do your show as you see fit. By the same token, they have the right to dislike it."

JASON: "What about instrumentalists? Miles Davis never responded to his audience in any way."

Truth be known, you don't have to do any of the things that I talk about here. If you are an exceptional singer or instrumentalist or songwriter, you can be as rude and abusive as you choose, and because you are so unique, people will withstand the abuse to get close to your genius. But how wonderful to be great and accessible, like Louis Armstrong, Kenny G, Paul McCartney, Bonnie Raitt. Genius in a caring, humane package. The best.

A little quiz:

"What is the difference between a good musician and a great musician? Between a good actor and a great actor? Between the good performance and the great performance?"

I won't leave you guessing. The difference is: When you're good, you know what to do. When you're *great*, you know what *not* to do.

GREAT
EXPECTATIONS

I'd like to spend some time on a most important word—a word that's used all the time in the entertainment industry, one you will hear more than any other in your career, by a wide margin. That word is *NO.*

How many times will you hear "no" before you hear "yes?" Of course, I don't have any hard evidence on this, but it seems to me that I hear "no" about twenty-five times for each "yes." No. No. No. No. No. No. No. No. No. No. No. No. No. No. No. No. No. No. No. No. No. No. No. No. No. Yes! Phew.

When a record company turns down your request for a contract, they say "No." Does it mean, "No, you're ugly?" Does it mean, "No, you don't have any talent? That your shoes are on backward? That your hair is too green?" No. *No* just means no. For that company, at that moment, you are not right.

How you accept somebody telling you "no" is going to make a big difference in your career. "No" is often painful. However, in the rinse of time, it can also emerge as a great kindness.

Have you ever met someone you wanted to know better? Asked them out, and been told, "no?" Ouch. Have you ever had someone who liked you, whom you didn't like back? They asked, "Could we get together sometime?" Your answer is "no." Not, "No, I hate you." Just "no." Then something interesting happens. The person to whom you said no starts pestering you to get together just once, or perhaps they say, "Hey, what's the matter? Don't you like me?" They refuse to lay off, and you are forced to hurt their feelings. "Go away and leave me alone." They didn't hear your earlier, gentle no, and their inability to hear this initial response forced you to anger and resentment, and to say something you didn't want to say and to be something you didn't want to be: harsh and unkind.

This is what happens when we refuse to hear "no." After being rejected by a record company, club owner, or most importantly, an audience, we may stay after them, making pests of ourselves, not wanting to believe they would turn us down. We may push. "Why wouldn't you hire me to play in your club? I think my music is pretty good. How about letting me open up for somebody?"

Or, instead of accepting with grace and sadness an audience's indifference or even outright rejection of what we have to offer, we start pushing. We hope—against all reason—that even though they didn't care for some of what we offered, if we push it all at them, they will miraculously change their opinion. Not likely.

People have various ways of turning you down. The best way is with a simple, clear *no*. But saying "no" is difficult for most of us. We hem and haw. We make excuses. We avoid the person. We duck and run—hoping they'll get the hint and go away.

If they resist, we are forced to use anger to get the point across. The residual resentment is most destructive. The inability to hear "no" brings out the worst in everyone.

"No" is a wonderful thing to be able to say. Quickly,

clearly, and without rancor. The best "no" I've ever received came from Clive Davis, a very fine record man and the head of Arista Records. Because I admire his "ears" so much, it's always been an ambition of mine to record for him. And to that end, I've sent him many demos over the years. The bad news is that in spite of my admiration for him, he has not heard in my music what he needed to hear to commit his company to my career. The good news is that instead of leaving me hanging, the rejections have always been clear and quick:

Dear Livingston:
Thank you for sending along your latest demo.
   Although it represents much fine work, I do not feel that any of the songs are particularly radio-friendly. As a result, it would be a most difficult project to market at this time.
   Wishing you the best of luck in the future.
Clive Davis

While "no" is not always that gracious, it is essential to learn to recognize the many ways people have of saying "no" and then to accept their decisions. Your ability to hear and accept "no" will vastly increase the number of times you hear "yes."

Also, try to understand that it wasn't easy for the person who had to say no. If you can do this, it says a lot about your character, which leaves the door open for an eventual "yes." Equally important, accepting the reality of a rejection allows you to move on.

This brings me to one of my favorite show biz truths. "If you haven't heard, you've heard," and the answer is "no."

That said, it's very tough to know how hard to push; when that one additional call may swing someone over;

when a touch of well-timed begging will crack the door. What do I recommend? Certainly one follow-up call or letter. Two, three? Be careful. Push, but avoid being obnoxious. Good luck.

Demo Tapes

Have any of you ever made a demo tape to get a record contract or club work? Sure, we all have. Demos are essential to the progress of our music. I like to view them as photographs, snapshots of my music at a particular place and time. Sometimes there are other musicians in my photo; sometimes not. Sometimes they're samples from a live show. Other times they're studio productions. Whatever you include in your demos, be careful about how much money you spend on them.

I've made demos for reasonable budgets, had them rejected, returned to the studio, and quadrupled the budget (up to $2,000 per song), expecting the quality to be four times better. It wasn't. Doubling a demo budget usually only improves its quality by five or ten percent. (And with each doubling, the percentage gets smaller.) It takes time to learn how to use a big studio budget. It's like giving a Ferrari to a student driver when a Hyundai would do.

Most importantly, avoid putting yourself in a financial bind when making a demo. If all you can afford is a cassette recorder in the middle of a rehearsal room, so be it. It's better than nothing and much better than being in debt.

I like to play my demos and watch people's reactions. Obviously, friends and family are going to tell you they like your music, but don't listen to them, watch them. Do they drift away as they listen? Also, watch for something else as you play your demos—how *you* feel. Are you comfortable or ill at ease? Pleased with what you've done, or wondering if you can fit under the couch? Now, obviously this changes all the time, but patterns do develop. As I make new demos, I like to include songs that worked well on earlier demos. I add them to the new mix—improving myself song by song, rather than reinventing myself each time.

Record Contracts

We've come to understand that the quality of our career is directly connected to our relationship with our audience. With that as a fundamental, what's the basic tool we use to expand this audience, to expose our music to more people?

TREVOR: "A tape."

Precisely. A recording of some sort. A recording is what an audience uses to revisit our reality and our view of the world. It's a musical picture of us.

To get exposure for that musical picture requires both financial capital and promotion. This is where a record contract with a well-financed company becomes important.

Who's traditionally responsible for signing an artist to a major label?

LAURA: "An A&R person."

And A&R stands for?

As Laura nibbles her lower lip, I whisper to her, "artist and repertoire," which she confidently repeats.

Exactly right, Laura. An A&R person, in consultation with promotion and marketing people, traditionally signs a new artist.

For Sony to find, sign, record, press, ship, and promote a new artist costs about $250,000 before a single record is sold. And the chances of a new artist making money for the company are probably not much better than one in ten. If an A&R person signs ten acts at an average cost of $250,000 per record, it's possible for the company to spend $2.5 million before it starts getting any money back. This isn't to say that it's not worth it, because a hit record can make them tens of millions of dollars on that initial investment.

Since no one knows what's going to succeed (in spite of the all-knowing posture show biz people love to cloak themselves in), the dance that ensues from the point of first contact between the artist and the company to the actual signing can be bizarre and protracted.

A&R people tend to lose their jobs after four or five bad signings. Because of the unstable nature of their jobs, they are notoriously fidgety and noncommittal. They'll try to string you along to prevent you from signing with someone else, and, at the same time, they'll try to avoid a commitment because it will mean that they are perhaps one signing closer to losing their jobs. When A&R people lose their jobs, where do they go? To the company that just fired *its* A&R person. It's quite the circle, and an ever-increasing aspect of modern corporate life.

The reason why somebody is an A&R person in the first place is because they were probably instrumental in signing an artist who made the company lots of money. As a result, they have some goodwill to coast on. Subsequently, they have signed four acts that have lost the company $1 million. Now they are feeling the heat to perform. What does this mean to you? It means they are going to string you along. If they sign another act that doesn't hit a home run for the company, they're likely to lose their job. And to them, the odds are only one in ten that you will be that home run. So they tell their boss they have projects in the works (that is, keep those paychecks and expense accounts coming). Then they tell the artist that the company is just about ready to sign, that they are a couple of weeks, a big meeting or another demo tape away from a positive decision. This is a dance I've seen go on for years. The artist is put on hold and the A&R person remains both a big shot and employed. Most corrosive of all is the artist's loss of focus on their audience as they attempt to please a corporate power structure. You do not have to play this game.

Instead, you can write a letter to the A&R person telling them that you are flattered by their attention to your music and that you will be expecting a record contract offer in a reasonable time frame (sixty days), and that if a contract is not forthcoming, you will consider their silence to be a de facto "no." Be forewarned. For this to be effective, you have to be willing to hear "no." Some prefer hope, regardless of how tenuous, to reality.

My favorite human quality is hope. It truly does spring eternal. There are two things you can bank on: Hope always triumphs over experience; and its dark correlate, Greed always triumphs over cynicism. ("Nobody ever wins the stupid lottery. I'll take two tickets.")

What Were They Thinking?

The reason why I speak about this A&R person is to get you in the habit of being in other people's shoes. How do they feel? What motivates them? What's going through their minds? What are their fears? What are their needs? What problems do they have that you can solve?

The same attention that we've learned to give to our audience can be expanded to include record companies. (Not to mention all the other people who are going to interface with our careers.)

The only reason to sign with a major label is their clout in getting you wide distribution and radio play. If major labels say "no," do not despair. There are plenty of other ways to get your music out there, including small labels, independent production companies, self-production, and promotion through the Internet.

Although I'm notoriously poor at predicting the future, the self-promotion possibilities of the World Wide Web hold wonderful promise. But do not delude yourself. You can't do it alone. You will need partners with expertise and influence to expand your audience.

Trust Me, We Really Love You

A record company signs an artist for two reasons. The first reason is that they love the music and believe in the quality of the artist. The second reason is a bit darker. The company is scared that if they don't sign you, somebody else will, and you will be successful for that other company. You can't imagine how deep this fear is among record companies. The A&R people who passed on the chance to sign Celine Dion or Dave Matthews live with that burn for a long time.

Often you are signed for a combination of both reasons—love of your music and fear of a competitor's success. It's unlikely anyone would admit to themselves that they were signing an artist out of fear, but I can tell you it does happen.

How do you know if you are being signed because someone likes you and your music or because they are scared you might do well for the competition? *It's impossible to tell.*

So a record company signs you, but the situation at the company changes and they release your album without enthusiasm. Business relationships have a nasty habit of going sour with amazing speed. Calls go unreturned. You fall off the face of the company's planet. Down the street is another company that thinks you are the greatest thing since car wax and they want you to record for them. They are psyched, you are psyched. Regretfully, when they learn that you are under contract with another company, they will say only one thing: "Get in touch when you are free." This is the worst situation you can be in. Bound to a company that's lost interest. This environment destroys careers. However, there is a way you can protect yourself.

Contract Essentials

All contracts must have two things. One, a performance clause. And, two, a termination date.

THE PERFORMANCE CLAUSE. Your voice, your arrangement of notes, your melodies, your lyrics, your energy. These are all tangible things that, when exchanged with an audience, can generate money.

I ask Boris, What does the standard management contract normally take as a percentage of the artist's gross income?

BORIS: *"Fifteen or twenty percent."*

Correct.

Now, what does the standard management contract say the manager will do for the artist?

CHARLOTTE: *"Help with the career."*

Jason?

"Get the band work."

Phil?

"Do the business stuff."

That's what you'd expect a manager to do, but what the contract says is usually quite different. The common phrase used in management contracts is "the manager will use his or her best efforts to further the career of the artist." Unlike the fifty to twenty percent the manager garners, "best efforts" is virtually impossible to quantify. When you sign this contract you have done something very common and very unfair. You have given away *something for nothing.*

I think this is important, so let me make up a bit of an example. Let's say Sarah McLachlan's management likes you. They think you are great. They think you can become a big star. They want to sign you to an exclusive management contract. You flip. Wow! Look at how big Sarah is. She's huge! If you could have just one-tenth of her career, you'd be set for life. Big time, here I come. So you sign with Sarah's management for an exclusive three-year deal with unending options. You agree to pay twenty percent of your gross receipts. What does management agree to? "Best efforts." You are giving away twenty percent and they are giving away "best efforts." If the relationship goes sour, drag "best efforts" into court and see what happens. Again, if you sign that contract, you are giving away something for nothing.

Ask questions like this: "So you think I have potential? What kind of money can I expect to make in a couple of years? Really? That much? That would be wonderful. Tell you what. Why don't you put into our contract that if I don't gross one-tenth of what you think I'm going to gross, our contract will end."

Reward enthusiasm, but be sure to outline specific performance levels that both parties must show for the relationship to continue. *Never give away something for nothing.* (From the business side, an artist overestimating their own worth is equally common and problematic.)

TERMINATION DATE. All contracts must have a termination date. That is, a date on which the contract is over, regardless of whether the terms of the contract have been met. Early-career contracts are notorious for containing self-renewing clauses when various terms of the contract are not lived up to. Self-renewing contracts are like quicksand. The longer you stand there, the deeper you sink.

For a young career, the longest time a contract should last is three years. Let me repeat: *three years.*

So, again, here are my two contract rules:

1. Never give away something for nothing.
2. Never sign an open-ended contract.

Since this advice seems so clear and easy, why do so many people sign so many terrible contracts? Because they are afraid. They panic, believing that if they don't take this deal, they will never get another chance. Their fear tells them there is only one star in the sky. This is not so. There are other relationships out there. Your quality will be recognized and it will shine. Don't give yourself away.

Take Me, I'm Yours

Arnold, ever mindful of the street side of life, asks: "Livingston, do you ever worry about someone ripping off your songs when you send out demo tapes?"

No. How wonderful to be such a great writer that somebody would actually *want* to steal your songs. I think it would be fine for a stolen song of mine to become a hit record. If you've got what it takes to write one great song, then you've probably got what it takes to write another. Why would someone settle for one stolen song when they could work with the writer and have access and control of dozens? Frankly, the biggest problem I have is people *not* wanting to steal my songs. When I hear of Stevie Wonder or Paul McCartney being sued by a schoolteacher in Minnesota for song theft, I shake my head. These are great songwriters. The schoolteacher sends them a demo tape, and when a song sounds like something they sent, they assume it was stolen. It wasn't. It wasn't even listened to. (I personally get a hundred or more unsolicited demo tapes a year. I can't imagine the shopping carts of demos Stevie Wonder must get.)

People are fascinated by anyone who is successful in their chosen field. Send them a demo tape, if it makes you feel better, but remember: The only way to a successful career is to find and develop your own audience.

Let's Play

Remember Dustin? He played a difficult classical guitar piece, his nervousness caused him to stumble, which made him more nervous, and the tension was excruciating. When he started to play an easy blues, his shoulders relaxed, and he looked across the class and smiled. The tension was gone. The joy returned.

Dustin was at ease and confident with this piece. He smiled, we smiled. He felt good, we felt good.

Once again, always try to play within your limits. Well within your limits. Performers are terrified that if they don't show everything they've got immediately, the audience will escape or think less of them. Don't let your insecurity and panic force you to attempt to spear your audience and reel them in. It's much better to hypnotize them with rhythm and seduce them with affection and discipline. I say this over and over because it is such an important part of performing. Do not go beyond your comfort level. Do not ask your beautiful music and talent to do more than it can. You will find yourself resentful of your talent when it doesn't live up to your inflated expectations. Said another way, your music is fine. It's your expectations that need some work.

Phil steps onstage with his guitar and plays a simple folk song. He makes a mistake and his face takes on a pained expression. Small mistake, big pain. He is beating himself up for being imperfect. And, as we've seen before with Krystal, beating yourself up for being human scares an audience because they're human, too.

If perfection does not make a successful career, what does? As I've thought about this point at various times, I realized I needed a definition of success before I could figure out what a successful career was. I looked for a common thread in the lives I admired. It didn't seem to be about money, power, or fame. Success seemed to be about *gratitude and thankfulness.* The ability to recognize that your presence here on the planet at this time is a miracle and nothing more need be expected or offered. Gratitude is success. Success is gratitude. They are interchangeable. Self-acceptance, forgiveness, and gratitude are very attractive qualities onstage.

Trevor gets onstage with his guitar, fiddles with the sound, tunes a bit, and then announces, "I guess that's good enough." When he finishes the piece I take exception to the phrase "good enough." Trevor, I say, that phrase tells your audience you're settling. It is another way of saying "Don't expect too much."

Trevor, mildly miffed, challenges me. "Okay, what would you do in the same situation?"

I walk to the stage, pick up his guitar, and fiddle around a bit. I look out at the class, stand totally still, and say one word: "Perfect." Now, everybody knows that the guitar isn't perfect, that I'm not perfect, and that the audience isn't perfect. So what do I mean by "perfect"? It is another way of saying that I believe nothing could be finer than this intersection we've come to, in sync and together. "Perfect." I like that word, and I ask Trevor to go along with me. "Fiddle with the guitar, look at us, and then say, 'Perfect.' " He does. The class cheers.

RADIO AND TV
AND THE
MAGIC OF "B S P"

What's B S P?

B S P is what radio and television give you. Let me sketch it out. You know how your girlfriend's mother thinks you're a bum? She's not exactly delighted that her daughter is going out with a disheveled musician when there are all those potential lawyers and doctors out there. Then one day she hears your music on the radio or sees you on TV and—ka-pow!—the world changes. Being included in the public airwaves has given you one of the pleasant rewards of show business:

B S P—Big Shot Potential.

Kidding aside, radio and television are essential to the expansion of our audience. We'll get to television in a bit, but let's talk about the most important promotional vehicle available to the early career: radio play.

How you get radio play for your music must be at the core of any conversation with a record company, because without radio play, it will be almost impossible to sell your music. Touring, press coverage, word of mouth, etc., all help, but nothing works like heavy radio play. Hundreds of thousands of people listen to a major radio station in an urban market at any given moment. To reach that many people by touring would require, literally, years on the road. When your music is played on the radio, it's a three-minute commercial for you. Imagine what Coca-Cola or Chevy pays for that same time, and you're getting it for free. (Uh, sorta.)

Let's look at the difference between radio and television.

What's your usual physical state when you're watching television?

Arnold: "Lying on the couch."

Do you watch TV when you're driving? Hammering nails? Flipping burgers? Jogging? Of course not. Watching television is a passive act. When you listen to the radio, you can be passive, but you can also do any number of things. Drive, work, study, date, sunbathe, party, shower. So you are living your life and the radio plays. The music on the radio becomes a *soundtrack for your life*.

Who gets transported to another time and place when they hear a certain song? Everybody. A girlfriend, boyfriend, a summer past, a group of friends, a job. Different songs remind you of different places. Sometimes it's the TV that connects a place to a song, but mainly it's the radio. I hear "Our House" by Crosby, Stills, Nash and Young and it's 1970 and I'm on Martha's Vineyard Island, a shy skinny kid, getting up the nerve to kiss a young woman upon whom I have a heart-stopping crush.

Or I'm at a truckstop south of Macon, Georgia. It's 2 A.M. and I'm eating eggs and toast after a week on the road. I'm tired and drained and completely available to be beat up by a song. And, boy, does it ever happen. It's a song I've probably heard twenty times before with no reaction. But now I'm ready and "Anything for You" by Gloria

Estefan, comes and gets me. It beats me up and slaps me around. Thump! Pow! Why didn't it do that the other times I had heard it? Because I wasn't ready. But at that diner on that late night when I was tired and lonely, it got to me, and I cried. I needed to cry and the song let me. It was the greatest. I was wet clay waiting for an imprint. Psychologically butt naked and ready to be branded. And Gloria got me because she and I happened to be together at the right place at the right time. I suspect it's happened to all of us many times with many songs.

In thirty years of making recordings and playing shows, I've done my share of branding other people. I see them come to my shows to relive these moments. I'm more than glad to help them retrieve these memories. Occasionally I'll watch an audience filing in for a concert and spot a person who is totally incongruous to my usual crowd. Perhaps a tattooed biker sort. The guy sheepishly finds a seat and I wonder why he's here coming to see me. And then I realize, I've branded him. I got him some late night in some vulnerable corner. Touching people with your music is the best.

This is a major component of the maturing career. We have become part of the soundtrack of people's lives. Our songs remind them of past worlds. And when they want to relive those worlds, they seek us out.

Branding people with your music is mainly the function of random chance. Your music happened to be playing when they were wet clay. They were ready for something and you were it.

Heavy rotation, that is, being played many times a day on as many radio stations as possible, increases the odds of your music finding a receptive home. Go for radio play. A song that's all over the radio is the definition of a "hit" record. It is *very* powerful.

Please remember: In every discussion with every department of a record company, include the question, "How are we going to get my music on the radio?"

How do you get your music on the radio? The person who makes that decision at the radio station is the program director (sometimes called music director). That said, let's talk about the normal hierarchy of a medium-size radio station. It includes: (1) the owner, (2) general manager, (3) program director, (4) sales staff, and (5) disc jockeys (on-air talent).

How does a radio station make money?

KRYSTAL: "Advertising."

Correct. Do you pay to listen to the radio? Of course not. You are a voyeur. You do not normally participate in any way in the course of a radio program. Although they desperately need you to listen, you are only indirectly responsible for their income. Advertisers finance everything. And how does a radio station decide how much to charge for an ad?

PHIL: "Ratings?"

You bet. There are companies that survey the listening habits of the population in a station's broadcast area. Rating points go up, money goes up. Ratings go down, money goes down. Pretty simple. If the ratings go down, and stay down, there will be changes made and someone will probably lose his job. The owner? I don't think so. The station manager? Maybe, but tough. Sales people? Never fire people who work on commission. That only leaves program directors and deejays. And the only one that concerns us here is the program director.

Program directors are the ones who make the decision to play our music. And they get fired constantly. They are the radio equivalent of baseball managers or record company A&R people. So, when you bring your music to program directors, again put yourself in their shoes. Give them reasons why they won't lose their job if they play your music and their ratings drop. Think about them in a meeting with their general manager justifying their play list. "Why did you play this Livingston Taylor record?" "Uh, I like his music and I think he's a nice guy." I don't think that's the answer an angry station manager wants to hear. You've got to show that your record has gotten a good response in other markets, that a local competing station has added the record and they are doing well with it. Show them that you've done public service favors for the radio station and are owed a payback. These are the reasons why program directors add records. If you can't give them these kinds of reasons, they are *not* going to play your music, regardless of how they feel about you personally. They've got to be able to cover their heinie in a period of down ratings.

Program directors receive hundreds of requests each week to add records. And why not? Your record, being played nationwide, is literally millions of dollars in free advertising for you. Sadly, I am not the only one who knows how valuable a hit record is. The competition for the few available slots is fierce. So what? Let it be fierce. I love it when the program director tells me he is going to play just two of the two hundred records he received in the past week. My response? "Who's the other one?"

Build solid relationships with program directors. Hear their needs, solve their problems, and get yourself on the radio. Although they regularly lose their jobs, they tend to be hired by the radio station that just fired *their* program director, and a positive memory of you travels with them.

If somebody is playing your record, write them, call them, thank them. Put yourself at their disposal. They are giving you free advertising. A letter might keep your record in medium rotation rather than light rotation, and that one extra play might be what's necessary to imprint one extra person. And, remember, once imprinted, they are yours for life. There is no unimportant radio play.

In the late seventies, I was promoting a song called "I Will Be in Love with You" and was scheduled to appear on several talk shows of the day—Mike Douglas, Merv Griffin, and Dinah Shore. I called my executive producer and main booster, Charlie Koppelman, and asked him, "Why am I doing these shows when none of my audience watches them?" He replied, "Probably not, but the mothers of the program directors of the radio stations we want to be on may be watching. Any leverage we can get will help."

When an audience is completely familiar with your music as a result of radio play and the subsequent purchase of a record, a wonderful thing happens. *They learn their part.* You play two chords at a performance and they know what's coming. They are completely at ease. You know the song, they know the song. You are free to communicate back and forth in a mutually understood language, the language of your hit record. It's a familiar and relaxed communication, and it's big fun.

My touring recently took me to the Old Town School of Folk Music in Chicago. A cold and the fatigue of the road had gotten to me, and my voice was failing. No panic, just a deep sadness that I wasn't going to be able to give my best. I started in on a song called "City Lights" and something wonderful happened. Because the audience was aware of my vocal distress and because they knew the song, they made a decision to help me out. I played the chords and they sang the whole song for me. I needed help, and they gave it to me. "Livingston, it's okay. We'll take this one!" A beautiful gift from a thoughtful bunch.

Now, getting a record on the radio in competition with the likes of Elton John or Billy Joel can seem like a daunting task, and indeed they have millions of dollars in assets at their disposal. But there is a higher truth than money. That truth is that a great record is impossible to keep down. A great pop record demands to be heard. It cannot be stopped. It will rise to the top. To again quote Charlie Koppelman, "To have a hit record, all you need is a great song and a tape recorder." And we all have equal opportunity to find the great song and record it. I believe there's a lot of democracy left in the Top Ten.

One of the reasons I am such a bear about record promotion is that you work just as hard to make a record that is heard by no one as you do to make one that's heard by every set of ears in the known universe. I make my records to be heard, and I want you to make yours that way, too. People worry about asking for too much. "I just want a sweet little career with a couple of people who love me"— as though their humility will mitigate the sadness of rejection. A fall from a small dream hurts just as much as a fall from a big one. It's okay to ask for the big enchilada. Somebody's got to have the number one record. If it can't be me, it should be you.

Moths to the Flickering Light

On to TV. First, I don't think much of television in spite of the fact that I watch a lot of it. TV is an enormously powerful tool. Treat it carefully. On TV, display the merchandise but don't give it away. By that I mean, don't play too much of your music. One or two songs.

Television can have an amazing effect on a career. If given in the right doses at the right times, it is *rocket fuel.* The problem is that performers start relying on it. TV is career cocaine. The second hit never gets you as high as the first. Television is to your career what white sugar and caffeine are to your body. A quick hyper buzz.

As a viewer, once you've surrendered to TV, it's difficult to duck out of the way of its images. (This is why advertisers love it so much.) When your image is on TV nothing is left to imagine. Television only shows the thinnest veneer of what you are. Because of this, it's very easy to become overexposed and boring. Far superior is the even "brown rice" of radio. There is no substitute for it. Radio is the background music for people's lives, and the more your music is played, the greater the chance that it will become the theme for a part of someone's life.

That said, you cannot avoid doing television. So learn how. Practice TV. Go on small local shows and check yourself out.

A couple of things I have found helpful regarding TV are:

1. If there is no makeup, use your shirtsleeves to wipe the oil off your face. A greasy face is most unattractive on television.
2. Avoid caffeine. The adrenaline of nerves hits the caffeine and it will be virtually impossible to play a coherent chord or sing an accurate note.
3. Begin counting the rhythm of the song long before you are introduced. Fifteen to twenty seconds is not too much. If you wait to start your count until the red camera light comes on, the rhythm is sure to suffer.

Don't Wet the Bed

Radio and television will not be enough. The bedrock of the career will remain live performance. Sadly, there are fewer and fewer places to play live music. Equally sad, some of the musicians who play in the dwindling supply of clubs often behave like groups they have read about in *Rolling Stone* and *Spin*: They are abusive and self-destructive. These magazines talk about this side of life because stories of drunkenness, destruction, and cruelty sell far more magazines than stories of normal, shoulder-to-the-wheel, clear-eyed work. But when a young group behaves poorly in a club by trashing the place—leaving behind a large mess and a small profit—the club owners may understandably give up and stop having live music. Listen, nobody knows better than me that small-time club owners can be unpleasant, but they do not deserve to have their establishments trashed. Bring the funky club up to your level. Don't descend to theirs. And *please remember:* That funky club may well be the last barrier between you and total obscurity.

Now let's play.

Jason sings and plays "Fire Lake" by Bob Seger. It is a good, well-known song. Although he is quite nervous, the quality of the song helps his performance. Because it is familiar to the class, it helps us understand where Jason is trying to go. A familiar song or "standard" is a good translator for your audience. When they hear your version of a song they know, it helps them understand your new material, the songs they haven't heard before.

This concept was brought home to me one day at my local police station. I was there filling out a form for a pellet gun permit. (No, I'm not a Ted Nugent wannabe. A red squirrel had taken up residence in my house, and the resulting destruction had driven me to a homicidal froth.) While I was standing at the front desk with a police sergeant, a Scottish vacationer came through the door, and when he spoke, he was completely unintelligible to both the sergeant and me. He spoke again, and again we were baffled. Although he was speaking English, his accent was so thick that we couldn't comprehend him. After three go-rounds, with ever rising frustration, he finally said a single word that we understood. That word was *direction.* Click. Instantly, we understood all. The one clear word made the accent intelligible, and we were able to determine what he needed—which, by the way, were directions to Wayland, the next town over.

The occasional familiar song can be the translation key to a lot of new ideas.

Charlotte plays guitar and sings a Graham Nash song. She holds the rhythm in her picking hand. The inevitable happens. The hand gets tired, and the more tired it gets, the more tension and pain there is. I have her internalize the rhythm and strum just the chords necessary to support the melody. The song immediately becomes settled and focused.

Again, the rhythm must be within the core of your person. It must be internalized. The music hangs on the rhythm like clothes on the body.

Boris sings while Jennifer plays the piano. I have Jennifer simplify by two-thirds the part she plays, and predictably, the panic diminishes and the focus increases. "Does anyone think less of Jennifer's playing now that she is playing less?" No, we like it more. So, if people sound far better playing less, why do they always try to play more? FEAR. The insecurity says, "I must play it all right now. If I don't, I won't get another chance. I won't be heard and I will disappear." The fear starts running the performance. So how do you quell the fear and stay within yourself? The short answer is, I don't know. It's different for each of us. I personally use prayer and spirituality for self-acceptance. An ongoing conversation with God might not help, but it can't hurt.

Krystal sings. Beautiful voice, pretty song. Her arms are stiff, her hands frozen. I ask her to resing the song using her hands and arms to help illustrate what is happening in the lyric. "Overdramatize, Krystal. Overdo the hand gestures for now. We can tone them down later." On the resing, the class much appreciates the way the arms help focus the lyrics. And although Krystal remains insecure, it is a big improvement. Watch Jane Oliver or Barbra Streisand work their arms and hands into their songs. If you've got it, use it.

Let's Play

We set up some microphones and start the day's performances. Laura steps up to the mike, and yells, "Check, one-two, check."

"Laura, is that your performance?" I ask.

LAURA: *"No, I just wanted to make sure the mike was working."*

Instead of yelling "check, one-two-three," why not lightly sing "check one, two, three?" It will give you a much better sense of how the system sounds. And if people are in the hall, it will make them laugh.

Kathy asks, *"What if people are there? Should they be cleared out during the sound check?"*

I generally think not. Let them watch the process. Acknowledge and include them. Make them feel that they are now insiders, because, as insiders, they will have a vested interest in your show going well. Also, it's less work to include them than to kick them out.

Charlotte sings a Suzanne Vega song. It's keyed a little high and with a whole tone reduction it's much improved. Pay close attention to the key as it relates to your voice and lyric. A little change can help a lot.

Okay. Who brought that bucket? I want to hear that bucket next. A tall, gangly fellow steps up.

"Hi, I'm Tim and I'm gonna play a bucket." Racket and bedlam ensue. When Tim's finished with his "bucket sonata," Phil and Kathy express confusion about the end of the performance. It's particularly important with the avant-garde or unfamiliar piece to first use stillness, then a bow, to define the end of the performance. It's unsettling for an audience not to know when to clap.

Remember, when you get through playing, the audience often doesn't know how you did. Their reality is still suspended and they're looking to you for information. With a light smile and pleasant countenance, you nonverbally inform them that what they heard was good, and although it might have been strange and new, they can go ahead and like it.

I pass out teacher evaluation forms and leave the class. For my students, it's *payback time.*

DOING WHAT
YOU HAVE TO DO

TIM: *"Livingston, is that you singing the Little Debbie snack cakes commercial?"*

"Yes. Do you think it's a bad idea for me to sing commercials? Does it cheapen my voice? Does it mean that I've sold out?"

TIM: *"I don't know. Maybe a little."*

I used to think it would be wonderful to make a living doing only the things I wanted to do. But I discovered a pleasant reality while doing the things I *had* to do. It's the things we have to do that take us to magical places. The early-morning flight to Newark, New Jersey, that forces us to be up before sunrise, and puts us in a position to witness the miracle of a brand-new day.

I have a small airplane, and sometimes when I fly to a show the weather on departure will be terrible—not dangerous, mind you, just crummy. Rain and turbulence. I'll take off into that mess, and as I gain altitude, the rain diminishes, the clouds above me lighten, and then, all of a sudden, I break out into a crystal-clear world of sun and blue. I am the only person in an unseen world above the clouds. And it is *so cool*.

If I had had my way, I would never have rotated into that mean sky, and as a result, I would have missed the miracle on the other side of the clouds.

The things we have to do lead us into unseen worlds filled with new things to become passionate about.

I try to be careful in judging other people's use of their talent to make a living. *Please remember,* when you're starving to death all food is health food.

I sang that commercial for Little Debbie because, with a certain quantity of earnings through the SAG-AFTRA union, I get my health insurance paid for. Also, singing and writing music is what I do and if Little Debbie snack cakes wants my music, they can have it.

I see myself as a crafts person, not an artist. As long as it's not too corrosive or destructive, I'm glad to give it my best shot. Also, what I will or won't do very much depends on the situation I'm in at a given time.

A number of years ago, I was making a CD called *Life Is Good.* I was broke and needed $25,000 more to finish the project. I was just about to borrow the money by taking out a loan against my house, when an ad agency called and asked me to sing a beer commercial. I explained to the agency that I didn't feel very good about using my music to promote beer sales and that I was probably going to pass. But before I did, I asked how much they were willing to pay for my services. The reply? Exactly $25,000. I found it remarkably easy to sit on my morals, sing the commercial, and use the found money to finish my CD.

Soft Pillow, Hard Floor

By the way, thanks to that found money, the CD came out, got radio play, and introduced me to a whole new group of people.

As my students and I spend more time together, I confide in them this reality: The performing arts are tough fare. I look at my students and explain that they are my competition. I want them to feel free to come after me. It will break my heart to be replaced, to be knocked off the top of the hill, but at the same time, I respect the tenacity required to get to the top. "Make no mistake. I want you to be able to take my place, but I am not stepping aside and turning it over. You have to come and get me."

Many times you'll find yourself in competition with others. Don't be suprised if the winning doesn't feel as good as the losing felt bad. Performers are often shocked when success doesn't bring the expected satisfaction. Winning is bittersweet at best. You triumphed over friends and colleagues who were perhaps equally qualified.

The illusion of life at the top is just that—an illusion. There's no certain point in your career where the going gets easy. The details in the struggle change, but the struggle remains. The acceptance of this reality will dictate how comfortable you will be with success and recognition.

I believe there are three gates through which you must pass on your way to recognition.

The first one's quite easy: Are you good enough?

The second one gets harder: Do you want it?

The third gate is the most difficult of all: Are you tough enough to get it?

Prayer

There comes a point in your career where all the conversation, rationalization, introspection, detachment, and observation do not work. You're moments away from being face-to-face with your audience, and in spite of your best efforts, you're sick with fear and nervousness.

There's only one place I've been able to turn for any relief at all. And that place is to a conversation with a force beyond my comprehension. I turn to prayer.

It took me a long time to get back to praying after it failed me as a young boy. There were five of us children, and when I was eight, my parents took us all on a summer trip to Europe. At one point, the three older siblings and my parents went to Italy for two weeks and left my younger brother, Hugh, and me in a youth hostel–type place in Switzerland. It was awful. The staff felt that my brother and I were little rich spoiled American kids (probably not an inaccurate observation), and they were determined to give us some good Teutonic discipline. Oh, how I hated that place. Each night, I prayed to God to have my parents return and rescue my brother and me, and each morning I was still there, my prayer unanswered. By the time my parents finally showed up, my relationship with God was toast. God was not there, not home; or, if he was home, he was too distracted to be dependable.

However, human beings must be able to call on the universe in times of need, so as time went on, I cautiously tried getting in touch with God again, to find ways to make God a more dependable ally. When nervousness and fear threaten to drown me as I take my place before some important career event, I love having a conversation with God. But what I enjoy saying is thanks. I thank God for putting me in a position where I *can* be nervous. If I'm nervous, it's because it's important to me. I asked for it. I asked to be in this place. I wanted to be at bat, and now I am. I've been given what I asked for. Pitch the ball. I'm ready for whatever happens.

God (like your audience) responds much better to gratitude than to complaints. And it's much easier to get good results from God when you don't get too specific (try not to request the color of the new convertible). Also, try to maintain an ongoing conversation with God. It's much harder to get a hold of somebody when you're in a panic if you don't have their phone number memorized. So a regular (read, daily) conversation with a power of your choosing is a bit like money in the bank. Put in those gratitude deposits, then when the heat gets on, you know just where to go for a withdrawal.

Try to remember that God is driving the bus. Make the occasional direction suggestion if you must, but don't forget to enjoy the view. And don't be surprised if the suggested turn doesn't happen. The universe is neither for you nor against you. It's completely indifferent. Do yourself a favor. Watch the universe instead of waiting for the universe to watch you. At the very least, you'll have more fun.

Autographs

When I was thirteen years old, I was walking across the campus of the University of North Carolina in Chapel Hill. It was a warm, late September evening. There was a concert going on in Memorial Hall, and in those pre-air-conditioned days, all the windows were open, allowing this amazing music to spill into the soft night. Curious and nimble, I climbed in a backstage window and, keeping out of view, was able to look over the band as they played to the audience beyond. Fronting the band was a very old man. After the curtain closed, he almost collapsed. When the curtain opened again, like magic, he was full of life. Closed, near collapse. Open, total energy! That an audience had such power fascinated me. (Even at that early age my report card suggested that I might poke around for a career alternative, and this audience/magic thing showed promise.)

At the end of the final curtain, the audience filtered out of the hall, and after a time the band leader/trumpeter left and began walking slowly toward his bus. I approached this tired old man and, filled with youthful presumption, asked for his autograph. He stopped, looked at me, and asked my name. I said, "Livingston." And he wrote, in the most beautiful, clear handwriting, "Livingston. Best wishes. Louis Armstrong."

When someone asks me for an autograph, time permitting, this is my routine. First I ask their name. "Jane." Then I say, "Is that . . . *J-a-n-e*?" *Never* guess at the spelling. Always double-check. If the name is misspelled, the autograph is useless. Then I write something like "Best wishes" or "Much love" or "Thanks for listening." I like to keep greetings simple and fairly conservative. When I sign my name, I make sure it's readable. When, and if, somebody shows my autograph to somebody else, I want that person to be able to read and understand the signature. One time I got Muhammad Ali's autograph. It was illegible. Understandable, as he was in the middle of a crush of people when he signed it. When I show it to people, I have to tell them whose autograph it is. As a result, its effectiveness is diminished.

Lastly, I date the autograph. When someone comes back to see me years later, it's fun to see the date. People remember the moment. The date keeps it clear when the moment was.

An autograph will not help your career in a big way. It's a small career thing that takes surprisingly little effort to do well. If done well, it will wind up on someone's wall and be a promotional vehicle for you for the foreseeable future. Everybody visiting that room and seeing the autograph will be regaled ad nauseum with the story of the encounter. I like to help my career in the big ways but find I have much more opportunity to help it in the small ways.

Hit the Road, Jack

Let's talk about travel and equipment...that is, the physical act of being on the road and the machines and electronics we use while we're out there.

When you are starting out, you and your band are going to spend a lot of time playing with used equipment and driving around in beat-up old vans. Why? Because that's all you can probably afford. Even so, there are things you can do to make the experience of using used equipment less eventful. Some thoughts on the old van:

1. Steam clean the engine and drivetrain. It is much easier to find and work on problems (and there *will* be problems) on clean equipment.
2. Replace all hoses, fan belts, and windshield wipers.
3. Change all fluids (coolant, brake, transmission, rear differential, engine).
4. Check the brakes and tires.
5. Buy a new battery.
6. Replace all burnt-out lightbulbs—not only for safety but also to avoid late-night encounters with bored police who love pulling over old vans that are obviously full of musicians. The burnt-out light gives them a reason to stop you.
7. Gaffer's tape (also known as duct tape), wire, and a Swiss army knife can solve a remarkable number of mechanical problems.
8. A cell phone is a nonnegotiable essential.

Be sure to leave early. Give yourself enough time for things to go wrong. Always travel as far as you can as soon as you can. Travel first. Rest later. Exception: Don't drive if you're exhausted.

If you're traveling by plane, fly early in the day. (The later it gets, the more delays are compounded.) If there's a mechanical delay and it's suggested that you deplane, always take *all* your carry-on belongings with you. Waiting to get back on a plane to get your stuff limits your options. Play the "I've got a show to do and people are depending on me" card. Remember, all is fair in love, war, and canceled flights.

Also, don't get stranded in small airports. Try and stick to big hubs. Nonstop flights are always preferable. When you fly, rent cars at your destination. Waiting for college students or club owners to pick you up is an invitation to adventure at best, but more often, to disappointment.

Please remember: You don't want to be in a vehicle with anyone who is crazy enough to promote rock and roll shows.

At baggage claim, open your cases and check your instruments. The earlier you discover a problem, the better the chance of solving it.

Change strings often and early. Don't fix broken guitar and microphone cords. Once broken and repaired, they will always work fine until the most critical part of a show. Throw them out and buy new ones.

Just a mention about wardrobe on the road...I like to change my clothes just before I go onstage. I have to be careful about what I pack because all the clothes I wear, I also have to carry. The fresh clothes get saved for the show. The next day, I often wear the shirt I wore onstage the previous day, but sometimes, if I've played in a smoky room, it's too funkasized to put on. Then it's either search the laundry bag or break out a fresh one. I generally have pants that I play in and pants that I travel in. With any luck, you can get a couple of days' travel out of a pair of pants. A tip for changing your clothes when the dressing room floor is so grotty you're worried that to step on it barefoot might result in unwanted pregnancy: Stand on top of your shoes.

To carry my clothes, I've found the Samsonite-type garment bag to be good and convenient. It hangs up easily in hotel and dressing rooms and is pretty accessible when opened up. Do not overpack. If you need it, go out and buy it. It will still be useful when you get it back home. If I wash socks and underwear, I hang them over the lamps in the hotel to dry. Be careful. Trashing hotel rooms is one thing; burning them down is quite another.

In terms of finding food to eat, I have little advice. A club sandwich with potato chips is hard to mess up. But when it's 2 A.M. and the only place open is the 7-Eleven or the Toot & Scoot, kids, you're on your own. Frankly, I don't want to know. A hint: Stay away from pickled eggs.

During the day's performances, Boris sings with a tape backup, and during the course of the song, the machine "breaks" (actually, I turn it off). Binding yourself to an inflexible computer program or tape guarantees that if there is a problem, the destruction of the performance will be total. Now, I've lip-synched my songs a number of times (the most memorable being two appearances on Dick Clark's *American Bandstand*). I love the freedom of lip-synching, just being cool in front of the camera and not having to worry about lyrics or pitch or anything. But doing it live is high risk. Remember the first rule of the "technical": If something's going to break, it will always wait until you're most vulnerable.

Again, wherever you are going, arrive early to leave yourself time to solve problems. And when you travel, to paraphrase King Edward VIII, never pass up an opportunity to shower, rest, or go to the bathroom.

YAHOO!
SEX, DRUGS,
ROCK AND ROLL

Let's move to a discussion of two subjects that seem to pre-occupy most everyone: sex and mood-altering substances.

Let's start with sex, and the performance difficulties that arise when we attempt to use our sexuality beyond our own comfort zone.

Has anyone in this class, male or female, ever been exposed to sexual harassment or unwanted sexual advances as a result of performing?

Kathy responds, *"Sometimes drunk guys try to come on to me when I'm playing in a bar."*

"And Kathy, how does it make you feel to have some drunk slug come on to you?"

"Ugh. Nasty."

It's awful to be making your music and have people after you that you don't find attractive, people using your beautiful music in an attempt to exploit you sexually.

Our sexuality is one of the most important things in our lives. We need to be attractive to reproduce. It's wonderful to look in the mirror and feel that you're an attractive person with much to offer. However, we all have different comfort levels in terms of how much sexuality we expose; and those levels change dramatically depending on the environment we're in. The real problem comes when we use inappropriate sexuality in an attempt to advance our careers. An unbuttoned shirt, a provocative pose, the use of sexuality to get attention—it's a Faustian bargain. We want so badly to be noticed. We want our music to be heard.

It's more likely that this behavior will put you out on a high sexual ledge. Standing on a high ledge is bound to leave you tense and ill at ease. Overt sexuality has never been a substitute for exacting rhythms and disciplined melody.

Please remember: It's a lot nicer to wish somebody found you attractive than to wish they *didn't* find you attractive.

Rusty, a former student of mine, went with his band to New York City where they were scheduled to perform in a gay club. When he and his band mates arrived at the club and it was time to go on, the manager suggested the men take off their shirts. Rusty acquiesced but confessed to me that he felt cheapened and discouraged by appearing shirtless onstage. Some of his band mates, however, thought it was fine to be shirtless. What to do? Don't make this type of decision on the spur of the moment. If you have not discussed it, take the conservative path.

Sometimes I'll pull off my vest if I get warm onstage, promoting the occasional hoot from the crowd. I like to look at them and say, "Remember my age. Trust me. This is as far as you want me to go."

Mick Jagger, Tom Jones, Bonnie Raitt, Bette Midler, and Tina Turner are entertainers who use a large sexual component in their performance. Their apparent comfort with their sexuality is a source of both relief and amusement. They can turn it on and off because they are aware enough of what they're doing to know when the sexual innuendo is appropriate and when it's not. They are fully in control of this very nervous game. Their comfort in these areas is a result of years of experience.

On to booze and drugs. Imagine for a moment that you are going to consult a lawyer for the first time. You're welcomed into his office, and after the introduction, he nods, smiles, and asks to be excused for a moment. He opens his desk, pulls out a can of beer, pops the top, and chugs away. After a belch, he fires up a fat boy, inhales deeply, stifles a cough, exhales a cloud of smoke, and then, through glazing eyes and a purple haze, he asks about your legal problem. You wouldn't stay five seconds. This would be insane behavior from a lawyer, doctor, or plumber. For a band on a gig, however, this does not seem that far out of line.

How is it that a bus driver drinking a beer on the job will immediately be fired, and it barely evokes a second glance coming from a working musician? The arts are viewed as being rather undisciplined; wild and wonderful creativity can exist in some rather seedy and unfortunate places.

I'm reminded of a time early in my career when I was performing with a number of other acts at Howie Stein's Capitol Theater in Port Chester, New York. After finishing my short set, I joined a few friends in the audience. The group following me was a southern boogie band with an Allman Brothers flavor. The front man for the group was attractive and well dressed. Regretfully, he was also blasted. The extent of his excess became apparent to him only when he stepped up to the microphone and saw a large crowd all anxious and ready to be transported to some new place. Realizing his total inability to handle his responsibilities, he explained, "Hi, y'all. We were back stage gittin' ready and, uh, it looks like we mighta gotten a little *too* ready."

Frankly, I don't remember the outcome of his set, but I do vividly remember his total panic upon realizing that he had been called and was not ready.

Please remember: When you perform, you are responsible for the safe passage of your audience through your space.

You are the *designated driver*, the lookout, the early-warning system. In spite of what they say, your audience does *not* want you to party with them. If they perceive that you are out of control, responsible people will remain on guard, diminishing the extent to which they'll immerse themselves in your reality. Making them feel secure will allow them the freedom to totally involve themselves in your performance.

Jimmy Buffett is the ultimate designated driver. His manner is comfortable and relaxed and, at the same time, vigilant. Party your brains out. Jimmy's on the lookout, and if there's a problem, you'll be the first to know.

I was touring with Buffett in the early 1980s, and our travels took us to an outdoor show in Denver. Before Jimmy came onstage, members of the audience began throwing balled-up paper cups at one another. Jimmy, not liking the direction this diversion was taking, stepped on-stage and admonished the crowd to "knock it off," at which point, somebody threw one of these balled-up cups directly at him. As his face darkened, the audience froze in fearful anticipation. Jimmy scolded them like children. "Don't you EVER do that again," he chided with a pointed finger. The crowd, clearly sorry for their lack of control, wished forgiveness. It was immediately forthcoming. The incident was forgotten and the party/concert continued.

Headline News

Destructive behavior is far more fun to write and read about than good, responsible living. I personally love looking through the tabloids in the supermarket checkout line:

"Cher Has Sex with Alien Big Foot. Gives Birth to Drug-Addicted Siamese Green Peppers."

How much more exciting this is than an article on Livingston Taylor's average day: "Then Livingston took an early flight to Detroit, drove to Ann Arbor, and checked into his hotel, where he went to sleep for the afternoon. Fully rested, he executed a clean, sharp show, had a very mediocre meal at Denny's, called his wife to say good night, went to bed, and arose rested and ready to continue his tour." BOR-ING.

Publications like *Spin* and *Rolling Stone* derive a large part of their advertising revenue from tobacco and alcohol companies. Chemically induced destructive behavior is sought-after copy in these youth-oriented publications. The fact that some artists have had career success in spite of their chemical problems makes it easy to believe that chemical saturation is no big deal. It *is* a big deal. Make no mistake about it, the long-term success of people who abuse drugs and alcohol is the exception. For every band that does okay in a chemical haze, there are hundreds that, self-deluded, out of control, fearful and blind, drift into queasy mediocrity. Not my idea of great entertainment.

As for drugs, they are illegal. If you are caught with herb by an unfriendly police officer, you *will* enter the criminal justice system.

The criminal justice system will consume lots of your time and money. If you must take illegal drugs, be discreet. Don't take them in the company of other people, because when you stop taking them (and you *will* stop) you'll very much regret people having seen you get high, and memories of former drug environments will be a source of regret and embarrassment. In a focused career, there is little room for alcohol and drugs.

Fair Is Fair

Abstinence in the workplace allows you the clarity you need to respond to the ever-changing situations that are the only constant in an early career. For example, I was working in a small club in Cleveland a few Decembers ago, and it snowed the night of my show. As a result, the crowd was quite small. The club owner had guaranteed me $2,000, and had paid me a deposit of $500. He still owed me $1,500. At the end of the evening I went to his office to settle up. He had the $1,500 in cash for me. I asked how he did at the door, and he showed me $1,250 worth of paid tickets. I took his money, counted it, and handed him back the $750 difference between the contract price and what he had actually taken in at the door. He was stunned. He assured me that I didn't have to give him anything back, that he was good for his word (that is, his contract). I explained that neither of us could have predicted the snow, and for him to shoulder the entire loss was just not right. He gratefully (and quickly) took the cash. It's okay to give back money to make things fair. As your career progresses and there are more layers (road managers, agents, business advisors) between you and the harsh realities of show biz, try not to lose touch with what's happening to people in your name.

By the way, it works the other way. I was playing a show at the University of Maine at Orono, as one of three acts on the bill. The show was represented to me with a certain expected gross. The show did much better than expected, yet I was locked into the existing contract. I had no hesitation in explaining to the people involved that the circumstances had changed and that the deal was now not fair, and that my fee should be adjusted upward. They responded that a deal was a deal and it would not change. We have not worked together since.

Fairness rules. After the terms of a contract have been lived up to, it's okay to make an adjustment. It's not a sign of weakness to make a little wiggle room. When people get unfairly beat up, they either go out of business or turn vicious. Both are sad.

Again, sobriety vastly improves your ability to accurately perceive the environment you're in.

Dangers That Await You

What makes people desperate? The three most common offenders are sex, drugs, and money. In the entertainment business there is a lot of all three, so be careful.

I ask Phil about a rumor I've heard that something happened to his guitar.

PHIL: "Yeah. I left it in a friend's car on Saturday night, and when I got back from dinner, it was gone."

Oh, Phil, I am so sorry. I am crushed that someone would be so desperate and out of control that they would take something of yours that you both need and love. I wonder about the person who would inflict such pain. Phil, what's your mental picture of the person who did this?

"I don't know. Probably some drugged-out slug. I sure would like to find him and put some of the pain I've got back on him."

I bet. I wonder how this person views himself when he looks into a mirror. What does he see? A thief? A criminal? A miserable lowlife slug? Probably not. When looking in a mirror, I think we all like to believe that the person staring back is someone who tries to do the right thing. I'm amazed by the just-apprehended criminal on TV explaining why he shot the little old lady for seven bucks. "She shoulda done what I told her," he says, or some similar feeble explanation for why this terrible thing happened. Interesting logic. "I'm not bad. The situation was bad and I responded."

Now, are there truly evil people out there? Absolutely. However, truly evil people are a rarity, representing a minute percentage of the planet's population. The bad news is that if one of these people has their sights on you, you stand no chance. But, if such evil is rare, why are so many people getting ripped off, cheated, lied to, and generally set upon by their fellow man? It's simple. Good people in desperate situations do terrible things. So, for self-protection, what you need to be able to see is not evil people—because their evil is invisible—but desperate situations.

"Jason, step up here for a moment. Do you mind if I use you for a little experiment?"

"Ah, okay."

"Jason, you see yourself as a good person, don't you?"

"Yup."

"In looking at you I'm sure that's true. Do you have any siblings?"

"A younger brother."

"What's his name?"

"Zack."

"You like him a lot, don't you?"

"I sure do."

"Okay, class, let's pretend that I am the professor gone wild and I grab Jason's brother, Zack, and hold him hostage and I say to Jason, 'If you don't go and mug somebody in the next ten minutes, I am going to harm your little brother. Jason, do you believe me?'"

"Yes."

"Then get out of here and mug somebody quick."

Jason is off. He runs frantically into the street, hoping for a cop, but there is none and he's running out of time. He sees two big construction workers at an ATM machine with a handful of fresh money. He runs up to them and says, "There's a mad professor holding my brother hostage! To get him free, I need to mug you and take your money. Can you help me? Can you just give me your money?"

They think he's crazy and move away. Running out of time, he heads back toward the college and sees a little old lady with a purse on her shoulder. He explains, in desperation, "There's a mad man holding my brother hostage. Can I have your purse? I'll bring it right back when I get him free."

Her predictable answer to his panicky request is, "No," at which point Jason rips the purse from her shoulder, returns to the classroom, and frees his brother, convinced that he chose the lesser of evils to resolve a desperate situation, and that with the passing of time, all would be explained, understood, and forgiven.

Class, in ten minutes I turned Jason from a nice guy into a mugger. Is Jason a good person? Of course he is. But in spite of his goodness, a mock desperate situation drove him to mock criminal behavior. Let me repeat: True evil is, mercifully, rare. What we need to be able to see is not the evil person, but the desperate situation.

In show business it may be impossible to avoid working with desperate people, but if you are strong and clear enough, they will choose to go after weaker prey.

Looking Good

Let's spend some time on promotion, including press kits, photos, bios, and Web pages.

First, the press kit. A simple folder with your name on the front is fine. Keep it generic because, as facts about you and your band change, you don't want the folder to become obsolete.

On to the inside: photos. The more the better. What makes a good promotional photo? First, it should resemble how you and/or your band normally look. If you use your photo to make you something you're not (sexier, stronger, more hair, taller, etc.) it's a bit of false advertising. When people see the real you they will be, at best, confused. Be truthful in your promo shots. For example, it's sad for me to watch myself get older (more lines, less hair) in my recent photos. It is, however, what I am now, and it's truthful and responsible of me to represent what I am accurately (although I must confess I don't complain when a photo of a younger me pops up in some article). Keep the photos tight and close. The center and most important part of a publicity photo is the eyes. Keep heads close together. Pack in close and tight. If you're spread out, it's tougher for an editor to crop the photo (and crop they will) to suit their needs. A few color slides are essential to service the ever expanding technology of color print.

I ask the class, "Who pays for the newspaper or magazine in which your pictures will appear?"

TREVOR: "The consumer at the newsstand."
TIM: "People who subscribe."

The cover price of the publication contributes only a small portion to overall revenue. Far and away the bulk of revenue comes from advertisements. People pay money to get their products displayed in a publication. Let's say you plunked down a few hundred bucks to advertise your health food store in a small free flyer (the likely press available to the early career). The flyer's editor puts a photo of a band that looks like a group of scowling biker criminals next to the ad for your store. You'd flip! You'd call the editor, or the person who sold you the space, and complain. "Why is my ad running next to a photo of a band that looks like they're going to shoot somebody, then die of malnutrition?" The editor's probable response? "I'm sorry, it won't happen again."

Editors would have you believe that the sanctity of editorial rights would never be subject to the economic forces of advertisers. Nice fantasy, but I wouldn't count on it.

Smile and look relaxed in your photos. Okay. At least don't frown and scowl. Editors have space to fill; make it easy for them to fill that space with you. Keep photo backgrounds light gray, and without too much distraction. Nothing should take away from the faces. Avoid the temptation of goofy or gimmicky photos. Trust me, changing hairstyles and clothes will be the source of quite enough embarrassment twenty years down the road.

JASON: "Livingston, a friend of my mother's gave me a picture of you that she took in 1974."

As Jason shows the picture around, the class is much amused that their balding Brooks Brothers instructor had a heretofore unmentioned long-haired, pipe-smoking, hippie past.

At this point I have everyone in the class pull out various IDs of themselves, including driver's license photos. The photos are the source of much amusement and speculation as to what was on people's minds when they were taken.

When my driver's license photo was being taken, I had only one thought on my mind. I wanted my picture to say:

"Please don't give me a ticket. I'm very sorry you caught me speeding, and I'll be good from now on." Can a license photo get you out of a speeding ticket? I have no idea. Probably not. But at least it was a plan, a conceptualization of where and how this photo was going to be used. Details matter; go ahead and sweat them.

The biographical information about you and your band should be clear and to the point.

"Exploding on the musical scene, direct from a pulsating cauldron of symbiotic nuclear talent cones. . . ." Woah, stop. Watch the superlatives. (You might start believing them.) Just the facts, ma'am. Who are you, where were you born, where do you live, what are your interests? Accuracy and truth are your allies. Better to deliver more than promised, rather than less.

People become frightened that what they are is not enough; that they won't be seen; that the world will pass them by; so they tend to inflate who they are, and as a result, they stop being believable.

Please remember: Audiences are attracted to humility and self-acceptance. If you accept yourself the way you are and forgive yourself for what you are not, you will shine brightly indeed.

As discussed earlier, the only access an early career has to mass media is usually through local newspapers and small radio stations.

Many years ago I did a talk show with the syndicated advice columnist Ann Landers and, as you might expect, she gave me some advice.

She said, "Always be informative when you're on radio and TV."

Let me take a moment and explain why this is so important. People love to learn. People love receiving new information about how the world works, even when it has

116

no direct bearing on their life; they like to hear about how a song was created, or the context in which a lyric was written. If you cannot be informative about your craft, you will wind up talking about yourself and your personal life. Regretfully, personal lives are either salacious or boring, and constant conversation about yourself tends to reinforce self-centeredness; and, as we've discussed many times, the good career is not about you, it's about them.

Cher was recently making the rounds of TV talk shows to promote her new CD. I found it regretful that the only questions asked of a woman who holds a lifetime's worth of show business information and experience were ones related to her personal life.

One of the problems with a lifetime of fame is that you have to struggle to get the conversation off of you and back to what's important, like what you've experienced in your career.

Please remember: Personal lives, well lived, are boring.

Early exposure on TV may be pretty tough to get. Local radio will probably provide your first media exposure. Either way, be ready to talk at length about your band, your music, and what you're selling (CDs, concert tickets, etc.). Expect that the disc jockey interviewing you will not know very much about you and might well be irritated at having his/her routine interrupted to make way for you. Address the interviewer by name, making sure that the interview is not going to be edited in a fashion that will make using the interviewer's name awkward. Thank the radio station (use current ID style, for example, "MAGIC 106.7"), and make the interviewer look good. The general manager of the station may be listening. And don't answer a long question with a single syllable word: "I understand you and your band had quite an adventure recording your last album on location in the Baja region of Mexico."

"Yup." Ouch.

Always be prepared to play live. Keep songs short, sixty seconds or so. Try to listen to the radio station you're going to be on before you get there. Get a sense of the flow of the show (hyper morning drive, shock jock, or NPR pontification).

One time I was on my way to do a morning radio interview outside Pittsburgh. I listened to the show on my way to the studio, and it was apparent that the disc jockey was running a remarkably rude, and to my ears, offensive show. It was a hard spot to be in. When I got there I had to walk a fine line between promoting my music and not participating in his audience abuse. Frankly, I never found out how well I did. But at least I knew what I was getting into in advance.

Press Agents

Laura asks, *"When do press agents come into play?"*

Press agents are responsible for getting current information about you to the media and putting the type of spin you want on that information. This, of course, assumes that the press/media is interested in you. No press agent can get publicity for you if the media is disinterested (you can lead a horse to water...). Often, people hire press agents for a short time, pay them a lot of money, and get no results. Very frustrating. If you've paid a press agent too much money and then beat on them, they will get you press, but it will be junk: *National Enquirer* lies, free flyers in a grocery store, and the like. Not helpful. Build a relationship with a small publicity agent and don't overpay or you will have to end the relationship before it bears fruit. Start early and be patient. Good press takes time.

Jennifer asks, *"Livingston, who normally pays for this?"*

Sometimes you can write publicity into a record deal, but remember, the artist always pays eventually. You're borrowing money from yourself.

She asks, *"If the club where you're playing doesn't like what you sent out for publicity, will they put together something of their own?"*

Jennifer's naïveté is refreshing. I explain again that in the early career, if you and your friends don't do it, the chances are very good it won't get done.

The best exposure available for a new band is the World Wide Web. With the stroke of a key, all information about you is available to 5.5 billion potential consumers.

HOME SWEET HOME

New York, Boston, Seattle, Boulder, Nashville, Chicago, Bar Harbor, Los Angeles, Austin. The choice of where to live can have an important bearing on a starting career. Once a career is fully established, you can probably live anywhere you want. Although, for me, life in an urban area tends to offer up a palette of challenges, good and bad, that keeps the old brain hopping.

Cities offer a diversity of music partners, competing music stores, information resources, places to find an audience—bars, clubs, restaurants, theaters, streets, subways. Places to figure out the parts of you that interface well with the people who will be paying your salary.

Boris asks, *"What about New York? I think I'd like to live there."*

New York is a wonderful, exciting place with great opportunities, but it has problems. It is very expensive, and getting in and out of Manhattan to go on the road is difficult. It's hard to find enough space to safely store your gear. Parking is impossible. And a handful of guitars in a three-story walk-up or minuscule elevator is not fun. True, the best is there as well as the worst, and if you're tough enough to take it, the competition can push you to some high levels of competence.

The important thing is to live where you can sell your

music, where there is strong competition and where there are talented technicians (tuners, guitar repairers, recording engineers, arrangers, teachers). In short, live in or around a major city if you're planning on selling the things you create.

All major cities have one thing in common—mobility. It's called *good* public transportation, aka, the subway. A subway gives new ideas a way to get around and meet other new ideas.

Boris asks, *"Where does Paul Simon live? I love his music."*

He lives in New York City, but the reality is that he can live anyplace he wants. Why?

"He can afford to."

Why else? He's a songwriter. The person who creates has the most choices. The greatest strength is in the creative process, in the ability to make something new out of the familiar vapors that surround us. But the new creation, although wonderful, is not enough. You still have to market what you make, or it isn't worth anything. If you don't sell it, it has no value.

In 1977 I took a river trip in Alaska with a man named Evan Chouinard. He had just started a small company called Patagonia to sell outdoor clothes, but at the time he was mainly known for his many mountaineering inventions. He was a diminutive man who held his hands behind his back. When he spoke, which wasn't often, it was usually to remark that we had been lucky with the weather (a statement that was inevitably followed by pounding rain). As he had brought a number of innovations to mountain climbing, I asked him about inventing.

With a touch of resignation he replied, "The invention is not very important. What you invent must be marketed."

Selling what you create, although often unpleasant and occasionally painful, is nonetheless your responsibility. If you have other people sell for you, there's a good chance they will sell you and your art in a way that reflects their taste, not yours. Your face, their soul. Mmmmm.

As my brother James says, "Don't be afraid to accompany your art into the marketplace."

The biggest problem you face in hiring people to do the jobs you don't want to do is that it can put you out of touch. Always be ready and able to do the funkiest, most boring jobs in your career. (In the young career you have no choice.)

One time I was promoting a record in Japan and we had done seven straight hours of tedious promotional interviews. At one point toward the end of the day, a person from my record company said, "Are you tired yet?" I replied, "Are there any more interviews?" He said, "A couple more." I answered, "Then I am not the least bit tired."

Champion yourself with enthusiasm, and when you hire people to work for you, be careful about the demands you make on them. Good management requires knowledge of other people's abilities. That said, I must tell you that I, personally, am not a very good manager. I tend to push at people. Because I demand a lot from myself, I demand a lot from others. It's important to remember that in most circumstances people are already doing the best they can. I call this the "sausage principle." So named for an incident on the New York State Thruway.

It was midmorning and I was driving west around Syracuse, New York. I pulled into a rest stop and went inside to get some breakfast. The service was cafeteria style, meaning one woman served eggs and toast and then passed the plate to the next person, who placed either sausage or bacon on the plate. The plate was then passed to the customer to be totalled by the cashier. Pretty simple, but there was a problem.

There was a holdup at the sausage guy. He was a gangly young man, nineteen or so, and with great concentration and deliberation he would, with a pair of tongs, pick up a sausage from the pan and, one by one, slowly transfer that greasy bit of food onto the waiting plate. He was so slow that a backup of four or five people had developed at his station.

With my youthful impatience, I barked, "Yo, let's pick it up a little, okay? We've got some hungry people back here." My hope was to speed the process. The result? It slowed dramatically. The pressure of my wisecrack caused that fellow's hand to start shaking so badly that those tongs became a blur of random motion. Find a sausage? Forget it.

In my impatience, I had failed to consider that the fellow might be doing the best he could. When my temper gets short now, I like to take a bit of a breath and remember that kid with the wiggly tongs, the "sausage guy."

Fame

Be careful what you wish for.

People are remarkably unprepared for success. Their fantasy tells them that fame and income will bring them familiarity and peace. They are devastated to find that their fame brings them, instead, isolation and loneliness. This is why people at the top of their careers occasionally die. Janis Joplin. Jimi Hendrix. Jim Morrison. Kurt Cobain. . . . They were self-medicating, not to get high, but simply to try and feel better when the reality of their lives at the top bore no resemblance to the earlier fantasy.

This is what makes fame so sad. It was going to solve so many problems. If everybody knew you, you'd have the ultimate leg up in the gene pool. The fantasy of fame is so delicious. Did someone hurt or reject you? Did they make you mad by telling you NO? In your hurt, the fantasy bubbles up. "I'll be benevolent with my fame; I won't need to crush them. That they didn't hitch their wagon to my rising star will cause them agony enough." These are delicious escapes from perceived injustice. Sadly, it never works out that way. Fame that is generated by publicity machines, for example, television exposure, newspaper and magazine interviews, in-depth exposés, highway billboards, and the like is the worst. It turns you into a cartoon of yourself. Because you have been in their face, when people see you, they believe that they have a right to be in *your* face. They point and stare.

I was walking through a shopping mall at midday a few years ago when I saw a most attractive woman walking a perpendicular path to mine. As I slowed to admire her, she noticed me. Her face brightened considerably. Now, I'm not all that young or good looking, so the notion of an attractive woman brightening at the sight of me made me feel great. And then a most heartbreaking event occurred. After her face brightened and she smiled at me, she tapped her girlfriend on the arm and pointed. Sigh. Her attention wasn't human attraction, it was product identification. She recognized me. Now don't get me wrong. I know my job, and I know that celebrity value is part of the promotion of my art, but we need to be very careful about our private image. When I see actors complain about the intrusion of the paparazzi into their lives, I scratch my head and think, What did you expect? You sold your soul when you allowed your personal life to be used to grind out another drop of visibility for some mediocre movie. You demanded their attention when you wanted to further your agenda and now you expect to turn them off? Good luck.

Given this depressing scenario, why would anybody buy into this? Because there are wonderful things that happen when you and your art are accepted. The badge of fame, once you get used to it, gives you the ability to perform your art in the company of the very best professionals out there. Trust me. It's fun making music with the best players, in great studios, with wonderful arrangers, producers, and engineers.

Further, when people examine the kind of fame they really want, they come to realize that it's much closer to home than they thought.

To be known and respected by your peers as a crafts person and an artist.

To be recognized as a dependable professional.

To look in the mirror and see a responsible and loving sister, father, nephew, employee, boss.

To walk into a room of people you know, and see their faces brighten.

Now that's *good* fame.

Please remember: It's difficult to observe when you're being observed. Gratuitous visibility will hurt your powers of observation. Plus, when you're ill or injured, it's very nice to be able to disappear into your cave and lick your paw until you're well again.

View your own career as a little pod. You're on a journey and it's fun to take the trip with your contemporaries—your band mates, your audience, your personal manager, the road crew; those who are similar ages often have similar sensibilities and worldviews. Resist day-to-day guidance from old people. They will attempt to spare you the pain they have endured. The motive is good, but the task impossible. The pain and humor of your collective naïveté will be your bond as *you* get older.

When it comes to important life events, or when you're anticipating a long commitment, definitely seek age and experience for advice. Older record company owners, lawyers, producers, and teachers (in reasonable doses) are fine, with the caveat that their egos must be in check. Careers aren't damaged nearly as much by naïveté as arrogance.

Take Money Seriously

Making money and keeping money are wildly different tasks. When the art of your music and performance starts solving problems for people, you will start to make money. People gladly trade dollars for the relief of immersing themselves into the reality that you create. Wide acceptance of your craft can bring you a relatively large amount of money in a very short time. In spite of what the stupid state lotteries would have you believe, a radical change in income can be so unsettling that many artists will ignore, waste, or throw away this expression of people's acceptance of their work. Later they realize they could use some of what was wasted, and regret that they didn't set some money aside. Some suggestions:

1. Take finances seriously. This is one of the few places where mature advice can help.
2. Uncle Sam is your partner. Report your income and pay your taxes. An angry IRS *never* goes way. There is a statute of limitation on every crime except treason, murder, and back taxes, and you can declare bankruptcy to everyone except the IRS. Are you getting my drift?
3. Let me reemphasize, Uncle Sam is your partner. This also means he should pay his share. Find, and use, every possible legal deduction.

4. Own where you live. The tax relief and forced savings of owning a home are huge and important. Do not delay. Find a way to own where you live right now.

5. Fund retirement accounts to the fullest legal limit every year. Tax-deferred savings are incredibly powerful given a span of forty-odd years of work.

6. Be conservative. Don't get greedy. (Let somebody else make all the money, you make some of the money.) And how *did* the Mississippi get to be a big river? Many trickles. Finally, remember that beyond a certain point money is a wildly overrated commodity. If money made happiness, then Palm Beach, Florida, would be one of the jolliest places on the planet. It's not.

Before we start performing today, I want to talk to Phil about a tape he gave me last week. It had nice songs, good work. But I have a question: Why did you turn your voice down so much in the mix?

"Well, I'm not that great a singer."

"You're not Luciano Pavarotti, but you sound pretty good to me."

I like to turn up my vocals nice and loud. Why? Because it says LIVINGSTON TAYLOR on the front of the CD. I'm aware that I'm a good singer. I'm also aware that my voice has limitations. I cannot run faster than the speed of light; therefore, I cannot outrun myself. I have no choice but to accept what I am. To forgive in myself the things that I lack and work hard to improve the things that I have. Ultimately, realistic self-evaluation is so much more powerful than single, isolated pockets of talent. After honest self-evaluation, use your strengths to support yourself while you work on your weaknesses—think of Billy Joel, standing on his songwriting while he steadily works on and becomes a fine singer. Or Jimmy Buffett, standing on his magical audience-control abilities as he works on and develops his recording techniques. (Not to mention learning to become a pilot and successful author.) And although he does not sell as many records as he did earlier in his career, his current recordings are far and away his finest work. Go ahead and turn yourself up, Phil. Nothing is more attractive than self-acceptance.

In the mid-1970s I worked with an agent named Neil. He was starting to go bald and was very concerned about it. He asked me how I thought he would look with a toupee. I reflected on the question and, in a burst of clarity, suggested that "nothing looks better on a human being than self-acceptance." He paused, thought for a moment, and said, "Yeah, okay. But what about the toupee?"

Clearly, these spiritual issues are not for everyone.

Let's Play More

As the semester nears the end, I watch my students critique not only one another but also the shows and performances they attend—expressing mock dismay that this class has wrecked forever their ability to blindly follow a band, they see the whole in parts: some great, some rotten.

Laura performs a simple piece on electric guitar. She makes a mistake and instantly simplifies. The rhythm stays intact. She's learned how to throw freight overboard to keep the boat from sinking. She's learned *never to sacrifice time for technique.*

Tim is the next to perform. He's been a question mark for me the entire semester. Impassive, I have no idea of how much has gotten through. He sings an Eagles' song, "Tequila Sunrise." At the end of the performance his expression is neutral; his body, still; his eyes, observant. The class is comfortable with the stillness as they digest the performance. Tim bows slightly, signifying the end and inviting applause. An easy smile spreads over his face, saying both "thank you for your affirmation" and "I agree with your positive assessment." A perfect ending to a performance.

Applause is a gift. Receive it graciously.

Jason joins Tim, and they play a bucket and bass duet. It's different, and totally unfamiliar. When a performer does something unfamiliar, an audience relies much more on body language to tell them what's going on; and their posture, facial expression, and physical movement or stillness provide the glue that holds the audience to them.

Trevor steps forward to perform a piece on guitar. He's chewing gum. He quietly mumbles his name and then launches into a very fine piece of music. I ask about the gum, and a little fed up with my harassment, and knowing he's a fine player, he snaps, "The music should be enough."

I back off. Trevor has a point. The music should be enough. And, indeed, great players can abuse themselves and their audience and still people will come. But what a favor the likes of Louis Armstrong or Kenny G do for us. Great *and* gracious. Not forcing the people who love them to step through an emotional swamp to get close to the genius they crave. It's true, the wrapping can't turn a lump of coal into a diamond. But the wrapping does send an early signal about what's to come. The music should be enough; but, trust me, it's not.

Trevor swallows his gum and lays before us an easy, informative introduction about how his musical piece came to be. The edge leaves the class. The class explodes in applause, relieved that the tension has passed.

Jennifer sings a couple of songs, and after she's through someone remarks that when she started they were scared to breathe. Jennifer agrees that she, too, was scared to breathe. I remark again that performance is like a big game of Simon Says. An audience suspends their reality and enters yours. You hold your breath, they'll hold theirs. But it's hard to keep their attention when they're about to pass out from a lack of oxygen.

Krystal sings a beautiful gospel ballad to end the day's class. Jennifer accompanies her on piano. Aware of their limited rehearsal time together, Krystal sacrifices optimum stage position to be close to Jennifer, knowing that if you are close together you can point out problems to each other far more easily than if you're ten or more feet apart.

After all the cynicism, pain, and toughness that we spoke about earlier regarding marketing, fame, and money, the quality of their performance reestablishes why we bother.

SO LONG

The last class of the semester is always a melancholy time for me. I've grown attached to my students, and I'm going to miss them. I'm having separation anxiety. Was there something that I should have said that I didn't? Did I say anything too harsh? Was I tough enough?

I want them to do well. And by "well" I mean that I want them to drift through life with minimal fear and maximum gratitude.

When we're fearful, we're self-absorbed and boring. When we're free of fear, we're open to take in all that is around us. A big long continual drink of the universe. What fun to not know it all. To *not know nuttin'*.

I'm getting dumber. When I was twenty I knew everything. It was the high point, the tip of my comprehension. I've been getting dumber ever since. Here in my late forties I now know a couple of things on a few subjects. But I can't wait until I'm old enough to finally know nothing about anything.

I love Thomas Edison's frustrated exclamation, "We don't know one tenth of one percent of *anything.*"

How wonderful to observe the world without a preconceived idea or prejudice. To understand that our time here is rare and brief, and that anything that distracts from our ability to absorb is tragic.

My best shows are when I'm rested, wide-eyed, and neutral, wet clay ready to be imprinted for the first time with the completely unique experience of a new audience. Four thousand plus times onstage have taught me only one thing for sure: You can never be sure. Any preconceived notion about what a performance will bring will be wrong. You cannot know what will happen until you are at the intersection that is the start of a show. Each performance is a brand-new ride. Occasionally, on the way to an important or unfamiliar performing environment, my wife, Maggie—becoming nervous for me—will suggest performance ideas. Invariably, after a flood of thoughts, she'll look at me, smile and say, "You're not going to do any of this, are you?" To which I usually answer, "I don't know. I'm not there yet."

When you get there and it's not what you expected, please resist the urge to turn your back on your audience in any way. When it's late and they are drunk and sparse, and you are tired and frustrated, it's easy to blame them for your black hole. Try to remember that you work for them. They don't need what you're selling; they buy it because they want to. The fewer of them there are, the better they should be treated. They are the only thing between you and obscurity. It's not their fault that you are feeling desperate. They are your employer; they deserve your affection and complete attention.

"Don't Take It Out on Us"

In the early 1980s I found myself, not for the first time, without a record contract. In 1978, through the wisdom and energy of Charlie Koppelman, I had been taken to Epic (CBS) Records and had had a wonderful run that included two albums, a Top Forty single ("I Will Be in Love with You"), extensive tours with Linda Ronstadt and Jimmy Buffett, and shows with Fleetwood Mac, Air Supply, Pablo Cruise, a large blast of TV exposure—Merv Griffin, Mike Douglas, David Letterman, and *American Bandstand,* lots of press, two tours of Japan, and, in general, very fine and supportive treatment by powerful, traditional music industry forces. As I did not generate the profit levels for these companies that their attentions required, by 1981 they had begun to loosen their embrace and distance themselves from me. By 1983 I was again on my own and bumping along the bottom. The dreams and fantasies had been so lofty that it made my life out of the corporate embrace seem very low indeed. I was ripe for a lesson, and someone was about to take me to school.

The classroom was during my second show in a small, dingy club in New York City. The lights were crummy, the sound was poor. It was after midnight, and the club was probably one-third full, and in this little dive that meant twenty or so people. I was onstage and fuming. Oh, how the mighty had fallen. My bitterness was adding a palpable stench to what was already a pretty funky place, and yet those twenty-odd people hung in there. Love or stupidity? Who knows. Then came the lesson. At one point, during a pause between songs, a person in that small crowd, in spite of their love for me, had had quite enough of my attitude and decided to give me a well-deserved suggestion. Out of the darkness, in a clear, quiet, conversational voice, came their advice: "Livingston, don't take it out on us."

Aaaah! It was as though I had been kicked by a mule. Yes, I was in pain. Yes, I was fatally infected with bitterness, but I didn't think it showed. But it did. You cannot hide onstage.

Many times since that night I have had occasion to look out over small, unenthusiastic audiences and turn my knee-jerk reaction of disappointment back to the memory of that night and that bittersweet lesson: The audience is not the problem. They are the solution.

Arnold asks, rather out of the blue, "Livingston, have you ever gotten a bad review?"

Suspecting a personal agenda, I probe and find that some harsh words were recently written about a band Arnold was in. I told him how sorry I was because I know how much bad press hurts.

When the press gets ugly it's sad and painful. Early in my career I learned firsthand Katharine Hepburn's observation about reviews: "A bad review is terrible, a good review is never good enough." As a result, after a few years, I learned to avoid the press. The damage of a bad review is much greater than the advantage of a good one. Anyhow, I was doing a show in Cambridge, Massachusetts, that was being promoted by a guy who had to be my biggest fan. He deeply and sincerely wanted good things for me. The show sold out a couple of weeks in advance, and the promoter wanted it to be a real triumph. Unbeknownst to me, he started calling the *Boston Globe* to get them to send a reviewer to cover the show. Because he was so fond of me he couldn't conceive that others might not feel the same way. After much haranguing, the *Globe* finally agreed to send a reviewer. The show was, for me, a wonderful event. The review did not reflect my postshow enthusiasm. I got trashed. As I read the review—I always read things written about me; people who say they don't should be handled with care, as they are proven liars—I was devastated and confused. After about a day, the confusion left and I became incapacitated by anger. Of course, I was angry at the reviewer; but as well, I was furious at my promoter, who was also my friend and supporter, for throwing a rock at this hornet's nest in the first place. Later on, I saw a fan who had been at the show and read the review. He seemed very puzzled. He thought I was good, yet now the review put his good feelings about me in question. Because of my own damaged condition, I was hardly in a position to be of help.

My anger lasted almost two months. Two months of deep, incapacitating pain. Mercifully, the anger subsided, and after it had, I was able to learn a great deal: When you get a bad review, please remember that, just like you, the reviewer is doing his or her job to the best of his abilities. It feels personal. It's not. They don't know you. They are doing the best they can with the information they've been given. And, as we've discussed many times, it's okay to allow their view of you to break your heart, but don't allow their opinion to put you in that dangerous zone of anger and knee-jerk reaction. When people are uncertain about you because of what they've read, you can assure them that, although disappointed, you didn't take it personally and that it's okay for them, along with you, to disagree with what's been said.

That said, what kind of review would be good enough to overcome my basic insecurity? Perhaps:

Dear reader, when you read these words, I will be dead. But do not mourn me. Oh, no. For I die happy. Last night, I saw a performance that was so good I no longer feel it necessary to endure the burdens of this mortal coil, and can go to my reward full and complete.

Well, you get the idea. Let me repeat Katharine Hepburn's words once again for good measure: "A bad review is terrible, a good review is never good enough."

For my students, this last class is bubbly and exciting. The semester over, holiday, family, trips, and adventure lie ahead. I see them, but they look through me. Young people in a good mood. The best.

Lee plays a piece on his trumpet. It's good, and the class enjoys it. I have him pick it up again from the middle, and I start to sneak up on him. I move from my seat twenty feet away to within four feet of him before he notices me. "Why didn't he see me?"

BORIS: "His eyes were closed."
LAURA: "He was into his music."

It's great to be entranced by your own music, but don't go into that trance until you're sure the world around you is stable enough to withstand your absence. To emphasize the point, I have a casual conversation with Boris with my eyes closed, and a pained, soulful look on my face. It makes the class laugh.

Laura sings two songs with Trevor and forgets to introduce either herself or Trevor. She says, "I forgot. I'm too stressed out from exams." A perfectly reasonable excuse, but if people don't know who you are, how will they ever find you again? Remember, your name is important.

Phil and Krystal sing a Christmas song together. The song is familiar, and the feeling between them is good. At the end, Phil's face looks worried. A worried face is asking questions: "Was I okay? Did you like me?" Don't ask an audience to make judgment calls about you. In the main, they are good people and they'll be supportive. But, given their druthers, they would rather participate in your self-forgiveness than spend some of their own hard-earned forgiveness on you.

Our job onstage is not to ask whether our gift is good enough but to give what we can to the best of our ability. Let someone else judge its worth. And when the audience makes its judgment, accept it.

Jason and Jennifer perform a couple of songs, including "Under the Boardwalk," which Jennifer, playing piano, doesn't know very well. She attempts to mask her ignorance with a blizzard of notes. I have her replay the song using a third of the notes. All agree that simpler is better.

Charlotte plays a song accompanying herself on guitar. The guitar part is quite hard, and as the song goes on, more and more of her attention is diverted to her guitar hand because it's *getting so tired*. Lyrics, melody, time, all start taking a backseat to the burning buildup of lactic acid in the hand that is playing the difficult guitar piece. As I make a mental note to mention the building tension in her hand, she suddenly simplifies the part and the tension evaporates. Her slight smile indicates that she has, indeed, found a way to monitor herself and a way to rest.

"Livingston, it's tough when you hear something in your head and you really want to go for it."

"Yeah, it takes discipline to perform. Sometimes I'll hear Beethoven's Ninth Symphony, but I know better than to try it on an acoustic guitar." You don't get brownie points for crashing and burning. If you don't survive the battle, there's no chance of winning the war. Live to fight another day.

The semester ends with Tim playing a forceful avant-garde piece on the snare drum. Loud and raw, it's a bit of a forced march for the class, but Tim stands his ground and insists on our attention. Most all agree it was a bit weird, but good.

With a lot of handshakes and a couple of hugs, the class is dismissed with the knowledge that, as alums, they are always welcome back.

Did any of my thoughts come through? Was anything I said of value?

School is expensive, and I take the responsibility of transferring information very seriously. My usual class size is fifteen or so people. On the first day when I explain that the job of performing is not to put out but to take in, I watch, and usually three or four of my students light right up. They get it—from the first ten minutes, they get it. They sense the freedom that's possible if you're capable of observing and reacting rather than blindly spewing your noise into the universe. It's logical and credible, and they believe it. Passion with discipline. Wow.

What about the other twelve? As the semester progresses, I feel as though I get through and make strong progress with seven or eight of them. It's the last three or four that keep me up nights, searching for words that will explain and get through.

After the death of the semester, if they're ever curious to ponder what happened all that time ago, if a vague memory of the class comes into their brain but the details are fuzzy, I want them to have a place to turn. That is the reason for this book. It's okay that they're not thinking about me. They can be certain I'm thinking about them.

EPILOGUE
OR
WHAT MY
PIANO TEACHER
DIDN'T TELL ME

Good performance is about what you take in, not what you put out. It's about observing, absorbing, and understanding the environment into which you are placing your view of the world—this is your performance. Why didn't my piano teacher tell me this when I was nine? She didn't know. She believed that being good would be enough. And when being good wasn't enough, it meant perhaps that dark, unseen forces were at work. She also believed that there was a level of technical skill or magic beyond which nothing else mattered. Actually, she was right. Magic does happen. Sadly, the chances of that technical magic being available to anyone reading this are small indeed. Only one in millions are born with the magic, yet all of us must be heard to survive.

How will we be heard? By understanding the panic that can grip us when we're faced with the prospect of failure. By being aware of the deep danger we are in when we're in that reactive, panicked state. By knowing that the fear of failure will safely resolve into the sadness of unfulfilled hope. By believing that the pain connected with that sadness must not be given away or assigned with blame or bitterness. Owning your sadness makes you strong, and the strength gained increases your capacity for compassion. Compassion is the cornerstone of forgiveness and the ability to forgive is the best part of being human.

Unless you are sprinkled with magic, you're going to fail—early and often. Discouraging, harsh words come from people who can't own their own pain. They take it out on others. Your early failures of inexperience will be an easy target. Protect yourself. Stay focused. Put your head down and take a step at a time. Expect no improvement for at least two years, a time frame that helps avoid discouragement. Each new group you face will increase your experience. The weight of accumulated experience helps dampen the wild swings in confidence that torture the young artist. You will get better. You will improve. You will find your right size.

Always perform simply enough so that you have room to watch your audience. It is you who asked to be in front of them. They have the right to reject what you offer, and you have the right to let that rejection break your heart. Never be more ambitious for yourself than your audience is for you. Their desire for your success is heartfelt, and their affection for you is remarkably demand-free. So continual acknowledgment of their love costs little and makes you both feel great. In time, you and your audience's infatuation with each other will mature into deep mutual respect and affection. That relationship is a warm, even light on the sometimes dark path that people who perform must walk.

Livingston Taylor's career as a professional musician has rattled along for over thirty years.

He has toured—some might say, perpetually—with such major artists as Linda Ronstadt, Jimmy Buffett, Fleetwood Mac, and Jethro Tull.

He has recorded eleven albums, and currently maintains a performing schedule of more than a hundred shows a year, which include club, theater, college, and full symphony repertoire.

A strong television background includes hosting a daily syndicated pop music show *This Week's Music* for Viacom plus the occasional soap-opera cameo (reporter Sam Cocharan on the now-defunct soap *Texas*).

Now a full professor, Livingston has lectured regularly at the Berklee College of Music in Boston since 1985 and has taught a performance course there since 1989. The concept, and much of the inspiration, for *Stage Performance* come from those classes.

Born in Boston in 1950 and raised in Chapel Hill, North Carolina, Livingston is the fourth of five children of Isaac and Trudy Taylor. He was sixteen when he moved back to Boston to finish high school. "Barely," he says, noting that the next year he began performing in the Boston coffeehouse circuit.

At eighteen he met Jon Landau, who later became Bruce Springsteen's producer and manager. It was Landau who produced Livingston's first recording in Macon, Georgia, for Atlantic Records when he was nineteen.

Livingston has written most of his music repertoire, including such Top Forty hits as "I Will Be in Love with You" and "I'll Come Running"; and for his brother James, "I Can Dream of You," "Going Round One More Time," and "Boatman" (off the double Grammy-winning album *Hourglass*). In 1988 he received the Boston Music Award for outstanding folk artist.

He is the author of two children's stories, *Pajamas* and *Can I Be Good?* Both were published by Harcourt Brace.

Describing himself as a pop singer, Livingston also includes his guitar, piano, and five-string banjo in most of his performances.

"It's no mean feat, making a living as a professional musician for thirty years," he says. No mean feat. But to do it with style—ah, there's the beauty.

Livingston lives in a suburb of Boston with his wife, Maggie, and dog, Ajax.